An Introduction to Forex Trading – A Guide for Beginners

By Matthew Driver

Editor: Matthew Driver
Cover Design and Illustrations: Matthew Driver

Published by Wells Gray Press
Great Britain

Copyright © Matthew Driver 2011
All rights reserved.

No part of this publication may be reproduced, stored in a retrieval system, or transmitted in any form or by any other means electronic, mechanical, photocopying or otherwise, without prior permission in writing from the publisher.

This book is sold subject to the condition that it shall not, by way of trade or otherwise, be lent, re-sold, hired out or otherwise circulated without the publisher's prior consent in any form of binding or cover other than that in which it is published and without a similar condition including this condition being imposed on the subsequent purchaser.

Disclaimer

Investments in financial products are subject to market risk. Forex investments are highly speculative and any investment should only be done with risk capital. Prices rise and fall and past performance is no assurance of future performance. Accordingly, the author makes no warranties or guarantees in respect of the content. You should obtain individual financial advice based on your own particular circumstances before making an investment decision on the basis of information included in this book.

Investment lessons, comments and/or opinions presented in this publication are solely those of the author and contributors quoted. You are advised to conduct your own independent research before making a decision. In addition, you are advised that past performance is no guarantee of future price appreciation.

While we have tried to ensure that all of the information provided in this book is up-to-date and accurate we accept no responsibility for any use made of the information provided. You agree not to hold the author or publisher liable for decisions that are based on information from this book.

Table of Contents

Chapter 1: An Introduction to Forex Trading
Chapter 2: Forex Essentials
Chapter 3: Analysing the Forex Market
Chapter 4: Forex Charts
Chapter 5: Technical Trading Techniques
Chapter 6: Common Chart Patterns
Chapter 7: Moving Averages
Chapter 8: Indicators and Oscillators
Chapter 9: Fibonacci
Chapter 10: Trading Cycle
Chapter 11: Advanced Chart Patterns
Chapter 12: Timeframes
Chapter 13: Trading Strategy
Chapter 14: The Carry Trade
Chapter 15: Ready to Trade
Chapter 16: Trading Systems
Chapter 17: Some final thoughts

Chapter 1: An Introduction to Forex Trading

The Forex market can offer fantastic opportunities to traders from all walks of life. It is possible to make good returns on your investment, and many people successfully manage to turn their trading activity into full time jobs or good second incomes.

The chance to profit from the relatively small fluctuations and changes in the values of currencies means anyone can have a go at trading and with the vast array of conventional and online tools/applications that are currently available; it is relatively easy to get started, and begin trading.

Designed for Forex beginners, the aim of this book is to provide a comprehensive understanding of how the Forex market works, how it is possible to make profitable returns, and to introduce many of the technical terms and tools that are essential for everyday trading activity.

1.1 Early Warning

It is best to get the warnings out of the way, so that you are aware of them and can then decide whether Forex trading is right for you. As with any type of financial trading there are risks involved and it is important to understand these risks, as you can then develop strategies and learn methods that can help to reduce them.

'Warning: Forex Trading carries a high level of risk to your capital with the possibility of losing more than your initial investment and may not be suitable for all investors. Ensure you fully understand the risks involved and seek independent advice if necessary'.

It is likely that anyone considering trading in the Foreign Exchange (Forex) Markets will have come across the above statement, at one time or another and those that haven't yet, soon will. It is a warning that you will quickly come to recognise in the course of day-to-day trading and it is also an extremely important message to remember.

The truth is that there are risks associated with Forex trading, as with any type of trading, and it is important to understand and accept these risks, before progressing. Failure to understand the risks and prepare for what is involved with trading is likely to lead to financial losses. However, by taking the necessary time to learn and understand how and why the market works as it does, and acquainting yourself with essential trading knowledge, will considerably increase the chances of success.

There are many books and resources available that will try and tell you that they have discovered the perfect trading setup or offer promises of guaranteed returns. This is not one of those books! There is no 'magic setup' or 'guaranteed strategy' out there – as much as we all wish that there was! Even institutional trading houses with advanced quantification strategies, and teams of analysts will struggle to predict market movements correctly 100% of the time.

Forex trading must be approached in the same way as one would approach any other job. A successful trader is defined as 'one whose losses over the long-term are overall less than their gains'. Losses are a fact of life and every trader at sometime or other will experience them. The best tool available for maximising returns and minimising losses is 'market knowledge', and it is this that we have tried to encapsulate within this book.

1.2 What is the Forex Market?

The global *Foreign Exchange Markets* also known as *Forex* or *FX* represents the platform by which currency from one country can be exchanged into the currency from another. The value of currencies around the globe constantly fluctuate depending upon a whole variety of factors, and will range upwards or downwards depending upon the economic stability or instability of the countries which issue them. It is these fluctuations in value that present the opportunities to make money.

Put simply, this means that if a countries economy is performing well, then it is likely to result in an increase in the value of the currency of that country. Alternatively, if an economy is performing badly then this is likely to lead to a reduction in the value of that currency.

Key Lesson: Whilst there are obviously many different factors that can influence currency values, many of which we will consider later in this book, in simple terms the aim for traders is to identify when and how these fluctuations in currency price are likely to occur, and then trade accordingly.

1.3 Size of the Market

The *Forex* market is huge in size. Close to $4 trillion worth of currency is traded daily, making it by far the largest financial market operating in the world. Of this, approximately $1.5 trillion is traded by retail traders, trading the Forex spot market.

The total *Forex* market value represents many different activities, which will require the exchange of one currency into another. Businesses making overseas purchases or dealing with foreign suppliers and customers; international mergers and acquisitions; and, interbank dealing and transfers all require money to be transferred around the globe and converted into different currencies. This is achieved using the *Forex* markets.

1.4 Market Structure

The trading of stocks and shares is predominately conducted through centralised exchanges, which means that the price at which securities can be bought and sold, is controlled and manipulated by a few dominant institutions. There is, therefore, little opportunity to seek a range of prices for buying and selling within the market place.

The Forex market, however, operates using a distinctly decentralised structure. Many institutions and organisations can offer currency transactions at a variety of different prices. This means that there is the opportunity for a variety of quotations amongst dealers and the chance to buy and sell at a range of prices.

This type of decentralised organisation can initially seem confusing, however, by its nature, it actually provides considerable opportunity for retail traders. The competition that exists between institutions and market players actually ensures that the best possible pricing deals are available all of the time.

In the Forex market there is still a degree of structure amongst participants and it is useful to understand how the main elements of the market interact:

1. At the top of the Forex structure is the *Inter-Bank Market*. This comprises the world's largest banks and some of the smaller regional institutions that trade directly between each other using two standard systems; the Electronic Brokering Services (ECB) or the Reuters Dealing 3000 spot matching. Both these systems allow the larger institutions to transact easily between themselves, with minimal costs and maximum efficiency.

2. The next level of the structure comprises: *Hedge Funds; Retail Market Makers; and, Business Institutions*. This tier of participants utilise foreign exchange mechanisms, either as part of global business operations, or for speculative investment purposes. Operating at this level requires strategic partnerships, where transactions will generally be directed through commercial banking partners. As such, the costs participants incur, in order to transact, are higher than those experienced at the institutional level, but still more favourable than the terms available to most retail traders.

3. At the lower end of the Forex hierarchy are the *Retail Traders*. A diverse group, retail traders range from day traders who will trade everyday placing multiple transactions, to irregular participants who only trade now and again. The value of transactions at this level is equally varied, encompassing all budgets. Costs of trading are higher and the terms of activity less favourable since there are two levels above the retail trader charging fees on every transaction.

Access to the currency markets in the past was much more complicated and costly, but with the introduction of internet based retail brokerage it is now much easier to actively participate within the marketplace. **This means that there has never been a better time to begin to learn how to trade Forex.**

1.5 Forex v. Stocks

Many of the techniques used to trade the foreign exchange markets are equally applicable for the trading of stocks and shares. As a Forex trader you will find that the skills learned and developed in order to effectively trade, can be easily applied to trade other financial securities. Despite this though, Forex trading does have some distinct advantages over the trading of other financial instruments, particularly in terms of the possibility for larger returns on investments.

The main differences of trading Forex over stocks include:

- **24hr market** (No matter what the time of day or night you can trade around the clock owing to the global nature of the Forex market).

- **Commission Free Trading**

- **Liquidity** (The Forex market is extremely liquid owing to its sheer size. This means that there are always buyers and sellers active in the marketplace).

- **Stops** (Most brokers provide guaranteed stops when trading).

- **Leverage** (Traders can apply leverage to trades in order to maximise potential returns).

- **Identifiable Trends**

- **Easy access to Market News**

1.6 Making Money from Forex Trading

The objective for anyone trading the foreign exchange markets is to exchange one currency for another, in the hope that the price of the currency bought will increase in value, compared to the value of the currency sold.

The way this is achieved in Forex trading is through the use of a **currency pair**. A trade will always be based upon two currencies, known as the *currency pair*. This is because every time you make a foreign exchange transaction you are essentially buying one currency and selling another. Each pair will always be presented in a similar format. The first currency in the pair is known as the **base currency** and the second known as the **quote currency**. Together these form the basis of the exchange rate so that when buying, the *quote currency* tells you how many units of that currency are required to buy one unit of the *base currency*, and when selling the exchange rate tells you how many units of the *quote currency* you can receive for every one unit of the *base currency* sold.

The exchange rate described by the *currency pair* means that the *base currency* provides the basis for all transactions. Therefore, if you were to place a **buy** order for the GBP/USD (British pound/United States dollar) you would be buying the *base currency* (GBP) whilst simultaneously selling the *quote currency* (USD). Conversely, if you were to **sell** the same pair you would be selling the *base currency* (GBP) whilst buying the *quote currency* (USD).

Key Lesson: In order to make a profitable trade, you would **buy** the *currency pair* if you thought that the *base currency* will increase or appreciate in value in relation to the *quote currency* over the period that you hold it for, or, you would **sell** the *currency pair* if you expected that the *base currency* will depreciate or decrease in value relative to the *quote currency*, over the period.

1.7 Currency Pairs

In practice, when currencies are paired, then the one that performs better over a given period will rise relative to the other. It is the movement of these currency pairings that forms the foundation for making profits or losses on investments.

The format in which currency pairs are presented can be seen below:

1.8 Forex Majors – The Commonly Traded Pairs

Listed below are some of the major currency pairs and their abbreviations. A number have alternative 'nicknames', which are regularly used by experienced traders and are useful to know.

EUR: USD   Euro - US Dollar (*Single Currency*)
GBP: USD   Pound Sterling - US Dollar (*Cable*)
USD: CHF   US Dollar - Swiss (*Swissy*)
USA: CAD   US Dollar - Canadian Dollar
USD: JPY   US Dollar - Japanese Yen
EUR: GBP   Euro - Pound Sterling
EUR: CHF   Euro - Swiss Franc
AUD: USD   Australian Dollar - US Dollar
NZD: USD   New Zealand Dollar - US Dollar

1.9 Official Market Open Times

The Forex market is a truly global entity offering the opportunity to trade 24 hours a day. The various major markets around the world open in accordance with their local time zones.

Market	Time Zone	
	London GMT	New York EST
Tokyo Open	0:00	19:00
Tokyo Close	09:00	04:00
London Open	08:00	03:00
London Close	17:00	12:00
New York Open	13:00	08:00
New York Close	22:00	17:00

1.10 When to Trade

Despite the Forex market being open 24 hours a day, there are times when it can be more advantageous to trade than others, particularly as a newcomer to the market. The best trading times relate to when there are high transaction volumes and intensive market activity.

Optimum times for this tend to be mid-week and when multiple markets are open. For example, it is generally better to be trading when both New York and London markets are open and overlapping, rather than trading when there is only access to one of the larger markets. This means that it is important to pick both the day of the week and the time of day that you feel will be most favourable in terms of market participants and transactions.

There are a number of times when it can be best to avoid trading altogether:

- **Mondays** (Markets often react unpredictably to weekend news and activity).

- **Fridays** often produce low volumes and market participation as traders prepare for the weekend).

- **Weekends** (There are vastly reduced volume levels at this time of the week. It can be a good time to prepare for the fundamentals of the week ahead).

- **Holidays** (National holidays have similar problems to those experienced at the weekends).

- **Significant News Events** (Although it is good to be prepared to take advantage of news releases, trading immediately after these events should be limited to more experienced traders).

1.11 Finding a Broker

To get started trading Forex it is first necessary to find a broker and this means finding a company that suits your specific requirements. The final choice will ultimately depend upon your individual trading needs, but it is important to have a few key thoughts in mind when initially searching for an appropriate broker.

As a Forex beginner, your brokerage company should provide an account that has all the necessary tools needed to learn, understand, and practise trading strategies. It should also provide an account that will allow you to make trades suited to your budget.

Ultimately, finding a good Forex broker comes down to effective research. Try and get personal recommendations from friends, colleagues or family who may already have accounts with a particular provider. The Internet is a great place to uncover reviews and recommendations from fellow Forex traders, which can help guide you in the right direction.

Key things to consider when looking for a broker include:

- **Spreads** – The tighter the *spreads* offered by brokers the better the potential for making profitable trades.

- **Accreditation** – It is important to look for a broker that is accredited by national regulatory bodies. Ideally, they should also ascribe to a recognised code of conduct.

- **Terms & Conditions** – You should fully familiarise yourself with the *T&C's* of a broker before signing up for an account. It is essential to know how a broker will administer your account and to fully understand your commitments to them.

- **Demonstration Accounts** – Most brokers provide access to demonstration trading accounts and educational facilities. You should make good use of these and fully understand how the trading platform works before making any actual trades.

- **Reviews** – There is an expansive community of Forex traders providing information and advice to beginners. Be sure to read the reviews and testimonials of experienced traders many of which can be found online.

Most brokerage companies will now offer online platforms designed to help administer your trading activity and to provide all the necessary charting tools, which will help identify transaction opportunities and trading strategy. Whilst it is still possible to administer a trading account without Internet resources, using telephone dealing etc, an online platform is rapidly becoming more and more essential to become a successful trader. This is mainly owing to the sheer volume of information, resources and help that the Web can offer both novice and experienced traders alike.

The charting software that most brokers provide free of charge to clients will become a vital application and provide the basis for all your subsequent trading strategy, so it is important to find a solution with which you are happy and comfortable. Having features that you can easily operate and understand will greatly increase the chances of spotting successful trading opportunities.

1.11.1 Types of Broker

There are two main types of Forex broker providing access to the market place for retail traders:

Market Makers - who determine and set their own bid and ask prices.

Electronic Communications Networks (ECN) - who use the best bid and ask prices available from inter-bank institutions, at any given time.

For most retail traders a mainstream commercial Forex provider will provide the best solution with tools suited for both beginners and for those with increasing levels of experience.

1.11.2 Rogue Brokers

The lure of quick profits and the promise of making serious money is always a factor for many people who decide to begin trading foreign exchange markets. It is important, however, to be aware of some of the more unscrupulous practices which have developed in order to part unsuspecting private traders from their cash. Scams and dodgy practices involving Forex trading have grown exponentially with the simultaneous development of Internet based trading. Problems to be aware of vary from simple *'transaction execution issues'* involving brokers being unable to execute your order requirements when and how you wish, to more elaborate scams and outright theft.

Having an awareness of these problems and the potential risks that can arise with brokers will help ensure that you are protected in your everyday trading activities. Monitor review/messaging boards online so you are aware of any problems that other traders might be having, as they happen. Always remember the old adage that if something looks too good to be true, it often is - beware of brokers that offer guaranteed profits or deals that seem to offer implausible returns. Finally, if you are trading online and find that trades are regularly inaccurately executed owing to 'technical or connection issues' then this may be a good sign that it is time to change brokers.

Above all trust your instincts!

In comparison to other financial market instruments, the retail foreign exchange markets are fairly loosely regulated and the levels of relevant regulation vary across different regions. Despite measures taken by regulators to try and improve this situation, it is the lack of operational directives that can lead to some of the problems traders encounter. It is important to know and understand the operating rules for your specific geographic region and to ensure that your broker is covered by the measures.

1.12 Opening a Trading Account

There are 3 main types of trading account available: *Standard Account*, *Mini Account*, and *Micro Account*. The type of account most suited to you will depend upon individual requirements. The main differences between account types are the levels of investment needed to initially fund the account, the size of currency amounts that can be traded, and as a result of both of these factors the level of risk associated with each trade.

Standard Account

A *standard account* is, as the name suggests, the most common form of account and provides access to standard size lots of currency ($100,000), utilising leverage of as much as 100:1. This means that under the rules of Forex trading you will generally be required to have an available minimum capital of $1,000 to be able to take advantage of leverage at 100:1. The $1,000 capital is the sum known as the account margin and will enable you to control a currency lot of $100,000. However, most brokers will require that accounts be initially funded with levels over $2,000.

The *standard account* means that when you enter a transaction every pip of movement can be worth the equivalent of $10. This level of gain can seem very attractive to novice traders, but some caution should be exercised in the use of a standard account. Whilst gains can rapidly accumulate, this level of leverage can similarly quickly reduce capital reserves and lead to substantial losses beyond the original stake, should the market move against you.

Standard accounts are therefore generally more suited for experienced traders.

Mini Trading Accounts

A *mini trading account* simply reduces the level of capital required to initially fund the account, and provides traders with the ability to trade in *mini-lots*, thus reducing the exposure to potential gains and losses.

Generally, a *mini-lot* is equal to $10,000, which reduces the level of investment required to initially fund the account as well as reducing the risk associated with each trade. Most *mini accounts* can be funded with just $500 or less and the levels of leverage can be as high as 400:1. The *mini account* is better suited to traders who are relatively new to the Forex market or for traders who are happy to test new strategies with relatively lower levels of capital.

Micro Trading Accounts

Micro accounts are the final type of conventional self-trading account available. Brokers often offer them as a method of encouraging traders to try Forex trading and to do so with relatively low levels of risk. A *micro account* provides traders with the opportunity to trade in *micro-lots* of $1,000. This further reduces the levels of capital required in order to fund and begin trading.

Managed Accounts

In addition to self-traded Forex accounts, it is also possible to experience the potential rewards that foreign exchange currency speculation can provide without actively trading. *Managed trading accounts* provide an option to have an account which is centrally managed by a Fund Manager who will make day-to-day trading decisions on your behalf, based upon your risk profile, and profit/strategic requirements.

Chapter 2: Forex Essentials

There are many terms used by traders that can at times make it seem like the market has a 'language' of its own, and these can be confusing when starting out. An understanding of this specialist terminology is a vital starting point for any trader.

2.1 Pips

The term *pip* is used in Forex as the method of describing the change in value between two currencies as they move either up or down.

For example, where the value of the GBP/USD moves from 1.5125 to 1.5126 then that incremental movement represents one *pip*.

The measured value of a currency will be usually represented to four decimal places and it is the movement of this fourth decimal place digit that is equal to one *pip*. For most currency pairs this is the equivalent of 1/100 of one percent or one basis point. Some brokers will report currency values to five decimal places and when this is the case then each movement will represent a tenth of a *pip*. This is sometimes also known as a *pipette*.

Every currency has its own value, and so to calculate the equivalent value of a pip there is a set process to follow:

.0001 divided by the exchange rate = *Pip* value

There are some exceptions in the valuing of *pips*, particularly in the case of currency pairs that include the Japanese Yen as these are often only quoted to two decimal places.

Brokers will calculate the *pip* value on your behalf, but it is useful to understand the underlying process, as it is ultimately this accumulation of *pips* that will influence the calculation of trading profit or loss.

EUR/USD **1.4745**

Pip

2.2 Leverage

Leverage is the double-edged sword of Forex trading. Whilst on the one hand it provides retail traders with the chance to make substantial profits from the currency markets, by exploiting only relatively small movements in currency prices, it can equally lead to situations where losses, if unchecked, can far exceed original investments.

Knowing the implications of *leverage*, how it works, and how it can be used effectively will, over time, prove to be extremely beneficial. This means learning to manage *leverage* in a manner that will give the best possible chance of making profits, but at the same time reducing the risks and possibilities of accumulating losses.

Leverage, by definition is the instrument that allows a trader to borrow and control much larger amounts of collateral, using only relatively small personal investment. Traders can enter transactions using this personal investment, that when *leveraged* is multiplied to give control of a much larger stake of currency. This means that profits can be made from relatively small currency price movements.

The important lesson to remember is that *leverage* works in both directions, therefore in the same way that *leverage* will increase the value of any profits; it can also rapidly multiply any losses.

In practice, *leverage* will be used every time that you execute a transaction order. When entering an order you will be required to select the level of *leverage* that you wish to apply to that transaction, and this will determine the amount of currency that you ultimately control. The amount of money that you personally have to put towards the transaction is known as the *margin*. This amount will have to be available within your account before a broker will execute the trade on your behalf.

An example of *leverage* in action:

Imagine that you have $1,000 that you wish to invest in a particular currency pair and you decide to enter a *buy* transaction, also known as *going long*. As you place your order the broker will give you a variety of *leverage* options, depending upon the type of account you hold. For this example, we can use a *leverage* level of 100:1. This means that your investment of $1,000 is multiplied by 100 giving you control of $100,000 of currency. It is that level of currency that is then applied to the trade and you enter the market theoretically holding that amount to invest. If when you close the trade you have judged correctly and the price of the currency has increased over the period, then that price rise is applied to the $100,000 rather than your *margin* amount of $1,000, thus considerably increasing the level of profit accumulated. Conversely, if you have misjudged the market and the price closes lower over the course of the trade then the same *leverage* is similarly applied to any losses. This would mean that you lose your *margin* investment and any accumulated losses over and above the level of the *margin*. *Stop orders* can be used to reduce your losses should the market move against you. This type of *order* will be discussed in more detail in later sections.

Key Lesson: A statement that you will encounter regularly throughout your trading experiences will be the following warning:

'This is a leveraged product and can result in losses which exceed your initial deposit. Trading Forex may not be suitable for everyone, so please ensure that you fully understand the risks involved'.

Forget this at your peril! By keeping this assertion at the forefront of your mind and applying caution every time you trade, then risk of financial losses should be reduced.

2.3 Lots

When it comes to actual trade orders the Spot Forex market is traded in *Lots*. *Lots* come in a variety of sizes including: *Standard*, *Mini*, *Micro*, and *Nano*, which are each made up of different amounts of currency units.

Lot	Units
Standard	100,000
Mini	10,000
Micro	1,000
Nano	100

Lots work using the principles of *leverage* that we have already discussed. They simply structure the specific amounts that can be applied to each trade. Each *lot* is constructed from currency units, which simply translates into real term values, therefore a *standard lot* consisting of 100,000 units can be equivalent to a controlling monetary value of $100,000, etc.

2.4 Margins

As previously mentioned in connection with *leverage*, it is not necessary to have an account actually funded with $100,000 in order to control a *lot* of currency with that equivalent value. Instead, following the application of *leverage* a broker simply requires you to have a percentage or deposit on account, to which this *leverage* will be applied when you trade. This percentage or deposit is what is known as the *Account Margin*. The value of this deposit will depend on the type of account held, the specific requirements of your broker, and your individual preference.

In the case of a trade using *leverage* of 100:1 then the *account margin* required would be a minimum of one percent. So, if you wished to execute an order for a *standard lot* ($100,000) at 100:1 then you would be required to have a minimum of $1,000 as a *margin* in order to proceed. Brokers will often require the account to be sufficiently funded above the *account margin* so that any surplus amount can be available to fund possible losses.

2.5 Bids, Offers and Spreads

When dealing with the pricing of currency in the Spot Forex market there will always be two prices at any one time for every currency pair. These two prices are known as the *bid* and *offer* price, and the difference between them is known as the *spread*. It is important to understand the difference between these two values, as they are a vital element of all trading strategy.

Key Lesson: The *bid price* will be the price quoted at which you can sell currency, and the *offer/ask* is the price you will be quoted when you wish to purchase currency.

The *bid* price will always be lower than the *offer/ask* price and it is this *spread* between the two prices, which allows brokers and market makers to profit from transactions.

2.6 Long and Short Positions

One of the most attractive features of the Forex market is the opportunity to make profits whether prices go up or down. This means that, as a trader, it is possible to accumulate *pips* irrespective of whether they come from upward or downward trends, greatly increasing the potential returns available and providing considerable flexibility for developing trading strategy.

When a trade is made, the term used to describe this is known as *taking a position*. If the trade is based on a transaction where the trader is predicting that the price of a currency will increase over the duration, then this is known as a *long position* or *going long*. Conversely, when the trader makes a transaction whereby they are predicting that the price will decrease over the duration of the trade, then this is known as a *short position* or *going short*.

2.7 Order Types

In order to execute either the purchase or sale of currency it is necessary to provide instructions as to the quantity and method with which a trade should be conducted. The combination of these instructions is known as an *order*. There are four main types of *order*, and it is vital to be aware of the nature and implications of each.

Market Order

The *market order* also sometimes known as an *unrestricted order* is an instruction to buy or sell at the best available current price.

This means that a trade will be executed immediately at either the current *ask price* or *bid price* depending on whether the trade is for a purchase or a sale. Therefore, if the *bid price* for GBP/USD is 1.5673 and the *ask price* is 1.5675 then, with a *market order* you would buy at 1.5675 and sell at 1.5673.

Limit-Entry Order

The *limit-entry order* is an instruction to buy at a certain level below the current market price, or an instruction to sell at a certain level above the current market price. Depending on the direction of the particular *order*, then *limit orders* can be further specified as either a *buy limit order* or a *sell limit order*.

This type of *order* can be used to ensure that you don't miss the opportunity to make a trade. They are also especially useful for executing a specific trading strategy, as they ensure that entry and profit targets can be set and executed accordingly.

Limit orders generally cost more to use than *market orders*, however the benefits to the trader often outweigh the extra cost.

Stop Order

The *stop order* is an instruction to buy or sell when the price reaches a predetermined level. This means that it can be used to set entry and exit targets for the purposes of limiting potential losses or locking-in profitable gains. The *stop order* is often referred to as either just a *stop* or a *stop loss*. The specific methods for using this type of *order* will be discussed in more detail later.

Stop orders are not always an absolute guarantee of getting specific entry or exit points. When there are sudden swings in price then your broker may only be able to practically execute the *stop order* at levels lower or higher than that which was originally expected.

It is important to read and understand the specific guidelines in relation to the execution of *stop orders* for your broker, as this will ultimately influence how you utilise them in your trading strategy.

Key Lesson: In practice, the *stop order* can be utilised to help ensure that profits are collected prior to trend reversals, or as an essential tool to limit the potential risk associated with each trade. Setting a *stop loss* below an entry point when *going long* on a trade will help ensure that should a situation arise where the price reverses then losses are kept to the absolute minimum. The opposite should be applied in a *short trading* scenario.

Trading Strategy: The exact locations for the placement of *stop orders* will depend upon the trading strategy employed. However, it is worth being aware that if the *stop order* is set too close to an entry level, then small oscillations in price may lead to a trade being closed prematurely. Therefore, it is sensible to set *stop orders* just below or above significant levels of support or resistance.

Trailing Stop

The *trailing stop* is a specific type of *stop order*, which moves in relation to fluctuations in price.

A *trailing stop* adjusts according to the direction of a particular trade, tracking the price of a currency. The result produces a *stop level* that is constantly changing in relation to price movements so that the point at which a trade could close is adjusted. This helps to lock-in profits and automatically reduce any losses which may occur should the price undergo a reversal.

Key Lesson: The *trailing stop order* is an essential tool for Forex traders and should be considered as an integral part of many trading strategies.

Trading Strategy: Should you decide to *go long* on the GBP/USD and buy at a price of 1.5780 then you could set a *trailing stop* at 20 pips (initially 1.5760). This will mean that, should the price move against you and drop through the 1.5760 value, then your *stop* would be activated and the trade closed. However, should the price increase, as you have predicted, then the *trailing stop* should track this value and increase correspondingly. Should the price continue to reach 1.5800 then the *trailing stop* would now be set at 20 pips below this new level i.e. at 1.5780. The level of the *stop* will continue to rise proportionally to correspond with any price rises. Should at any point the currency price begin to fall, then the *trailing stop* does not drop back but remains at whatever level it reached prior to the reversal, in this case 1.5780. The trade will remain open as long as the market does not move against you by more than 20 pips, at which point the trade would be closed. The overall result is that the majority of gains accumulated during the trade are *locked-in*.

Other Order Types

In addition to the four main *order types* there are a number of more unusual *order* categories that are more suited to experienced traders. It may be that you never have to use these particular *order types* but it can be useful to be aware of them. They include: *Good-Until Cancelled* (GTC); *Good-for-the-Day* (GTD); *One-Cancels-the-Other* (OCO); *One-Triggers-the-Other* (OTO).

2.8 Placing an Order

The exact procedure to follow when *placing an order* will vary slightly between brokers and different trading platforms. However, irrespective of the precise method, whenever you do *place an order* you will need to consider a number of common factors that will form the basis of your trading strategy:

- Select which *currency pair* you wish to trade.
- Decide whether you are *going long* or *short on* the trade.
- Check your analysis and ensure that you are confident of where the price could be going.
- Check indicators and tools to reinforce the strategy.
- Predetermine exit points (using support and resistance).
- Predetermine a profit target (don't get greedy!).
- Select an *order type*.
- Select the *lot* size.
- Manage the risk associated with the trade (this will be discussed in more detail in later sections).

This, or a similar checklist, should be always used before you make any transactions. By going through each stage methodically it will help structure the way in which you execute transactions and help prevent making mistakes. It serves as a *checks and balance system* which will help to analyse each trade from a number of perspectives prior to making any commitments.

Once an *order* has been executed then it is essential to monitor the trade and implement tools which will help analyse the overall performance. Effective Forex trading requires keeping a cool head in order to try and not act too impulsively.

Key Lesson: It is important to stick to a strategy. There will often be situations where you may hit your profit target and feel that by staying in the trade you have further potential to make money. Chasing profits can be dangerous and by staying in a trade longer than planned it can increase the possibility of being hit by price reversals. By closely monitoring trades and setting *stop losses* at appropriate levels these risks can be reduced.

Similar situations can occur in loss making trades where it can be tempting to stick with a trade in the hope that it will ultimately reverse. Set a *stop loss* and stick with it. Losses are a fact of life for regular Forex traders, but by ensuring that they are kept to an absolute minimum, over time, will ensure that you win more times than you lose.

Chapter 3: Analysing the Forex Market

Developing a successful trading strategy relies upon collecting information relating to the markets and understanding the corresponding influence that this information can have on currency prices. This requires learning methods to analyse the market and price conditions.

The common types of analysis available to a trader fall broadly into three categories: *Fundamental Analysis, Technical Analysis* and *Market Sentiment*. Each provides a different perspective of market conditions, using information from a variety of sources.

3.1 Fundamental Analysis

Fundamental analysis is the process whereby trading strategy is developed and then influenced using items of news and information, which have direct impact on economic activity.

The principle behind this type of *analysis* follows that when a country's economy is doing well then this success should generally be reflected by an equally strong currency. Similarly, when a country's economy appears to be performing less well, then this is likely to result in a weaker currency. The relative change that this economic strength has upon economies and currencies subsequently forms a basis for speculative trading.

The information that forms the foundations for this economic data is referred to as *fundamentals*. *Fundamental* data encompasses many scales from macro-economic news, relating to global far reaching events, to more localised national economic information. The ultimate aim of *fundamental analysis* is to use it to try and determine how specific news, reports and data releases will influence the currency markets and to determine what trends may appear as a result of these releases. By knowing how the market may react to certain events or news updates it becomes possible to plan trading strategy, which can then capitalise upon these potential movements.

The relevance and impact of individual news items on markets varies. Reaction to major economic news can result in significant market movements, whereas the effect of less important information will have more subtle influences on price movements.

There is a massive amount of information released daily that can be used to effectively plan and manage trades. Below is a list of the types of data to watch for:

- Employment Rates
- Interest Rate Movements
- Retail Sales Figures
- Trade Balance Reports
- Gross Domestic Product Information
- Inflation Reports
- Durable Goods Reports

There are many resources available, both in traditional media format and online, that will have detailed information relating to the scheduling of these news reports. Many online websites and forums will also allow you to activate specific updates that will keep you informed of all relevant releases relating to a currency of choice.

Key Lesson: Make sure that you know which news releases are due each week. It can be useful to create a diary of events that you feel may have significant influence, and then utilise this information in the planning of future transactions.

3.2 Trading Using Fundamental Analysis

There are some important points to learn when using *fundamental analysis*.

The effect of news on currencies is generally related to the difference between the expected results (which will already be priced into the market) and the actual results. If a news report is released which meets expectations, then there is likely to be little movement in the related currency. However, where results are significantly different from those expected then there is likely to be strong movement in prices as the market adjusts accordingly.

When hotly anticipated news stories are due for release, there is often a quiet period in the markets prior to updates. If the released information is unexpected and produces subsequent currency price movements then the changes in price are often rapid and short-lived. Therefore, when trading *fundamentals* it is important to be ready to react quickly in response to information updates.

Some economic information has greater impact on the market than others. News releases that can have a strong impact on market activity include:

- **Interest Rates** (Where interest rates are up then currencies tend to rise accordingly).

- **Employment Figures** (Higher employment rates mean more people in work, generally reflecting a stronger economy and an equally strengthening currency).

- **Gross Domestic Product** (Higher GDP suggests economic resilience and a strong currency).

Less important news releases include:

- **Retail Sales** (Still a good indication of economic performance).

- **Durable Goods Orders** (Provides a measure of manufacturing performance)

There are some factors associated with the trading of *fundamental* information which require a degree of caution. One example of this is that market volatility often increases considerably during periods directly following news releases and this can lead to prices changing fairly rapidly over very short periods of time. This rapid movement can also be accompanied by erratic price fluctuations. Depending on the execution rates of individual brokers, these fluctuations can result in *trade orders* being fulfilled at prices that are different from that which you expected, as the price may change during the time taken to implement a transaction. This situation is known as *price slippage*.

This volatility can also cause prices to swing between gains and losses, over short periods of time. You should closely monitor the market at these times and be aware of how this movement is affecting your individual trades.

Key Lesson: It is vital to fully understand the impact of fundamentals on the market. If you are new to trading, then it is important to take time to learn the impact of news releases before trading at these times, as markets can suddenly and rapidly swing in opposite directions, wiping out your profits. Many websites and information sources provide Forex news schedules and should indicate the relative importance of each. By using a mixture of these resources it is possible to gain a reliable indication of the likely impact each scheduled item may have on the market.

3.3 Fundamental Analysis – Interest Rates

Interest rates are one of the most influential factors relating to the value of a currency. An understanding of how *interest rates* are used by central banks in order to try and control economic activity helps a trader determine how currencies are perceived to be performing. Central bank decisions relating to *interest rates* are possibly the most important fundamental news items and should always be closely monitored.

The principle reason for *interest rate* adjustments by central banks is to control inflation, which means attempting to limit the rise in cost of goods and services within a region. Rapid inflation means that prices on everyday goods and services, commodities, etc are increasing too fast, and eroding the spending power of commerce and the general public. Whilst a degree of inflation is an accepted element necessary for a growing economy, when inflation increases too rapidly it can be harmful to economic activity. Therefore, central banks will attempt to maintain stable low level inflationary conditions, with the use of *interest rates*.

Key Lesson: In simple terms, the way this is achieved is that when there are high levels of inflation then central banks will often raise *interest rates*. This results in businesses and individuals saving more and spending less, thus resulting in **reduced** levels of economic activity and helping to reduce inflation. Alternatively, when *interest rates* are lowered then this tends to encourage people and businesses to borrow more and save less, which means **increased** economic activity.

Trading Strategy: In terms of Forex trading, the higher the interest rate acting upon a particular currency, then the better the chances of that currency strengthening over time. Currencies with lower interest rates are likely to have weaker currencies.

3.4 Fundamental Analysis – Interest Rate Differentials

It is possible to use the difference between the interest rates acting upon two currencies as a means of determining whether one currency may be strengthening or weakening against another.

Key Lesson: An interest rate differential that increases supports the higher-yielding currency, whereas a differential that decreases supports the lower-yielding currency.

3.5 Fundamental Analysis - Example

A good example of how *fundamental* elements can influence the movement of currency prices is to consider the importance of key central bank decisions. When a country's central bank makes critical decisions relating to their economy, there will always be a subsequent effect upon that country's currency and any connected currency instruments.

If the European Central Bank wishes to try and improve conditions to encourage export, then they may decide to sell euro holdings and resort to purchasing a non euro-zone currency like the US dollar.

The intended result from a move such as this would be a subsequent drop in value of the euro against the dollar meaning that it is cheaper for businesses within the euro-zone to export goods and services. Often the announcement of key figures relating to moves, such as these, cause traders to begin to pre-empt movement in prices, driving prices lower, meaning the market itself helps move the currency value lower.

Key Lesson: As a Forex trader it is important to be aware of announcements such as this example and to understand both, how the market may react in the short term i.e. to the announcement itself, and then also to be aware of the longer term implications for the economy. By having an understanding of how currencies can move, immediately and in the future, in relation to fundamental economic strategy, then you will be able to identify related trading potential.

3.6 Technical Analysis

Unlike *fundamental analysis*, which uses economic data and news information to try and predict future possible price movements, the process of *technical analysis* relies upon studying the actual movements in market prices as a means of identifying discernable trends and patterns from the data. The idea is that historical price patterns should provide an indication of future market fluctuations.

Essential to *technical analysis* is the observation and examination of charts plotting past price movements. These provide the basis for determining possible future movements, trends and fluctuations in the price of currencies, as well as vital information for planning and executing trading strategy.

There are many methods available to a Forex trader using *technicals* in order to analyse the foreign exchange markets. One element that is essential to all of these, and which will form the starting point for each process, is the ability to chart and understand price movements. By observing historical price data, the aim is to try and understand the levels that future prices may achieve. Charts can also be extremely useful for highlighting long and short-term trends, as well as revealing patterns in the information that can be used to help examine market conditions.

In addition to the basic presentation of price, information charts also provide many opportunities to apply mathematical and statistical analysis, which can further uncover essential trends and patterns. The identification of these chart patterns are key to *technical analyses*, as they illustrate the past, current and potential future movements in price and underlying market conditions. By using these as a trader, it becomes possible to plan where and when trading transactions should be executed, and to define the strategy behind each trade.

Technical analysis is fluid in its nature, meaning that as conditions change in the marketplace (which can happen rapidly or over longer periods of time) the analysis helps to breakdown this information and present a clearer indication of what is actually happening and ultimately what may occur as a result. To a trader this type of information is vital, as it helps to convert seemingly random fluctuations in currency price movement into discernable representations of underlying trends and patterns.

There are many different types of *technical analysis* ranging from techniques that require the identification of specific patterns within the price data, to others that rely upon mathematical manipulation of the data in order to produce tools that indicate when, and how, trading should be potentially undertaken.

Effective *technical trading* should use a combination of these analysis techniques, as this helps to reduce the risks of identifying false trends or false indications. Multiple analysis techniques applied to the same data at any one time will help to reduce the risk of losses and increase the likelihood of accurately identifying true trends and patterns.

At first glance, this can all seem complicated. There are varying degrees of skill required to learn each of the techniques and apply it to everyday trading activity. However, once mastered and understood, *technical analysis* will become an extremely useful and essential part of your everyday trading activity. Developing a firm understanding of the basics will allow you to build extremely effective trading strategies which, over time, will become increasingly more accurate as each new skill adds a degree of complexity that can be applied.

Key Lesson: Understanding the meaning and implications of past price movements is an essential part of any trading activity. *Technical analysis* provides the everyday tools necessary to help structure and manage the when, where and why of each and every trading transaction you make.

3.7 Fundamental Analysis v. Technical Analysis

Both methods of *fundamental analysis* and *technical analysis* are extremely useful tools when trading Forex. However, whilst some people develop trading strategies based solely upon only one or the other of these methods, this is rare. In most cases the two types of analysis should not be mutually exclusive.

Key Lesson: To become a successful trader it is important to understand and use both methods in order to provide supporting trade signals.

In practice, this may mean using *technical analysis* to first discover the underlying trends in a currency price and to identify patterns and indications of where and when to enter the market. This analysis should then be supported by finding news sources or market reports using *fundamental analysis* that provide further evidence to reinforce or negate the trading strategy. News items, relating to the strength of the economy for that particular currency, should confirm or deny the original analysis and may also identify key news events from the trading calendar, which could have further significant influence on the price movement.

By using the two types of analysis together the chances of something occurring by surprise and ruining an otherwise credible trading strategy are significantly reduced.

3.8 Market Sentiment

Whilst *technical* and *fundamental analyses* tend to rely primarily on raw data as sources for determining potential price movements, a successful trader should also learn to consider a third type of analysis which involves trying to judge overall *market sentiment*. This is the process whereby a trader will attempt to determine the thoughts and feelings of other traders and try to develop strategy based upon this group psychology. Whether market traders are *bullish* or *bearish* is a key factor when planning trades. *Market sentiment* is a difficult concept to measure and comprehend, however, experience will gradually produce the knowledge required to gauge this *sentiment* correctly.

Bulls and Bears

The term *bull market* or when traders are said to be *bullish* refers to times when there is considerable optimism in the marketplace giving rise to larger numbers of **buyers** than sellers. These circumstances will often be accompanied by strong price rises and significant upward market movement. By comparison, if conditions are such that the opposite of this is true and there is considerable pessimism amongst market participants then this is known as a *bear market* or traders are said to be *bearish*. These conditions will generally be accompanied by a greater number of **sellers** than buyers in the marketplace resulting in falling prices.

Chapter 4: Forex Charts

Charts are the key to effective technical analysis, and there are numerous ways of presenting Forex data. Charts to be aware of include: Line charts, Bar charts, and Candlestick charts.

4.1 Line Chart

Line charts are the simplest representation of currency price movements. A continuous line is used to link the closing price from the current session to the closing price of the preceding session. The data shown by this type of chart therefore has limited detail but can be very important for indicating rising and falling trends over trading sessions.

Key Lesson: *Line charts* are extremely useful for indicating general price movements in the markets.

Forex Line Chart

4.2 Bar Chart

Bar charts provide considerably more information than *line charts*, and are an extremely effective method of visually representing greater detail in relation to price movements.

Bar charts similarly link closing prices, but also simultaneously present opening prices, as well as highs and lows for the session. The top of each bar represents the highest price reached during the session, the bottom represents the lowest price and the horizontal lines to the left and right of each bar represent the opening and closing prices respectively. The overall length of the bar indicates the price range for the session.

In most charting software bars will be colour coded – green to represent a rising price and red to represent a falling price.

Each individual bar shows information for a particular session. The time frame for this session will be dependent upon the context of the chart but could represent a minute, an hour, or a day.

Key Lesson: Bar charts are sometimes known by the acronym OHLC or Open, High, Low and Close charts.

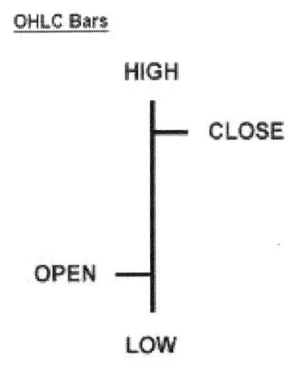

OHLC Bars

HIGH

— CLOSE

OPEN —

LOW

4.3 Candlestick Charts

Candlestick charts (often known as *Japanese Candlesticks*) are used to visually represent information relating to the price movements of a security, derivative, or currency. *Candlestick charts* are an important tool for Forex analysis as they encapsulate a large amount of information, and present it in an efficient and easy to read format.

Candlesticks represent the range of price movements over a given time period, making them ideal for technical analysis of currencies.

Looking at an individual *candlestick* it will usually comprise the body (black or white), and an upper and a lower shadow (called the wick). These upper and lower shadows represent the highest and lowest traded prices of a security during the time interval represented. The body illustrates the opening and closing prices. When the currency closes higher than it opened, the body is white or unfilled, the opening price represented by the bottom of the body and the closing price the top. When the currency closes lower than it opened, the body is black, with the opening price at the top and the closing price at the bottom.

Charting software will often replace the black or white of the candlestick body with colours such as red (for a lower closing) and green (for a higher closing), making it easier to visualise price movements.

4.3.1 Reading Candlesticks

Candlesticks are formed from the values for the open, high, low and close.

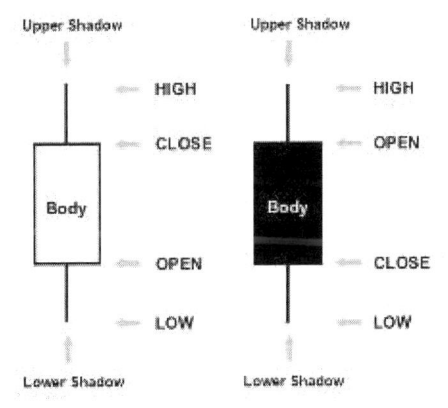

4.3.2 Long and Short Bodies

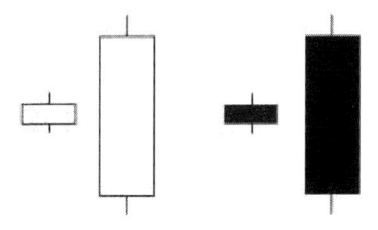

A *long white/green body* suggests a **strong buying** presence. Indicating that prices have increased considerably over the time period, the longer the bar the more significant the increase.

Conversely, a *long black/red body* suggests a **strong selling** presence indicating that prices have decreased over the time period, again, the longer the bar the more significant the decrease.

4.3.3 Shadows

Long *shadows* indicate that trading occurred well beyond the open and close prices, whereas short *shadows* indicate that the majority of trading occurred near to the open and close prices.

A long upper *shadow* and short lower *shadow* suggests that traders tried to push the price higher, but were unsuccessful. The opposite is true for *candlesticks* with a short upper *shadow* and a long lower *shadow*.

Candlestick Shadows

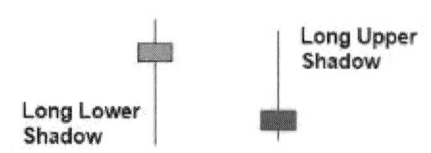

Long Lower Shadow

Long Upper Shadow

4.3.4 Basic Candlestick Patterns

Candlestick charts are an extremely effective method of illustrating the movement of currencies over a given timeframe. There are different types of *candlestick*, which can be used to determine the underlying trend in the market.

White/Green Candlesticks – suggest an **upward** trend in the market. The longer the body the more significant the overall price increase.

Black/Red Candlesticks – suggest a **downward** trend in the market. This time the longer the body the more significant the price decrease.

A *Long Lower Shadow* – suggests a **bullish** market (associated with increasing investor confidence in anticipation of future price increases). The main body of transactions are occurring at the higher price.

A *Long Upper Shadow* – suggests a **bearish** market (associated with decreasing investor confidence in anticipation of future price decreases). The main body of transaction are occurring at the lower price levels.

Spinning Tops – are *candlesticks* with long upper shadows and long lower shadows, with a relatively small main body. The colour of the body tends to be irrelevant as they indicate periods of **indecision**. The small main body shows that prices opened and closed within a limited price range, whilst the long shadows suggests traders have unsuccessfully attempted to push prices either up or down.

Maruboza – a *white maruboza* consists of a long white body with no shadows. It means that the open price is equal to the lowest price of the period and the closing price is equal to the highest price. It is an indication of **bullish** conditions. A *black maruboza* consists of a long black body where the open price is equal to the high of the period and the closing price is equal to the low of the period. It is a suggestion of **bearish** conditions.

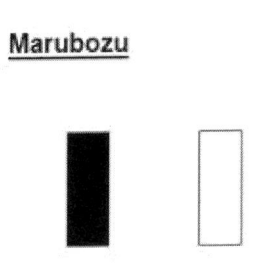

Marubozu

Doji – have extremely short bodies resembling just a line, where the open and close prices are either identical or extremely close. They suggest a lack of any significant movement during the period. If a *doji* forms after a sequence of *candlesticks* with long white bodies then this suggests that the demand amongst buyers is weakening. Conversely, if a *doji* is seen after a sequence of *candlesticks* with long black bodies then this is likely to suggest that confidence amongst sellers is weakening.

Doji Candlesticks

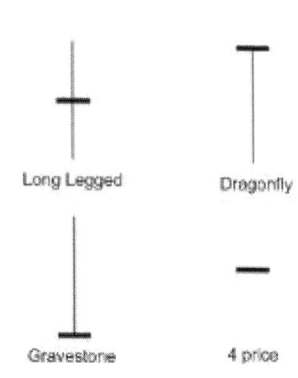

Long Legged

Dragonfly

Gravestone

4 price

4.4.5 Candlestick Trends

When using *candlesticks* for technical analysis, it is important to not always view them as individual entities, but to see them within the context of their surroundings. A single white/green *candlestick* following a number of black/reds by itself is insufficient to demonstrate a change in trend. However, should a number of white/green *candlesticks* begin to occur in sequence then this provides more significant evidence suggesting that a trend may be developing.

Candlestick Trends

There are a number of significant patterns that can develop within *candlestick* sequences, each of which can be used to identify possible price trends. In this book we will not examine all candlestick trends in detail, however, the diagrams below highlight some examples of the different types of candlestick pattern that can occur:

Tweezer Top Patterns

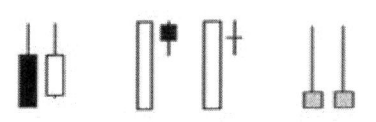

Tweezer top patterns can often be spotted towards the end of an extended upward or downward trend and suggest that prices are likely to reverse.

Three Black Crows

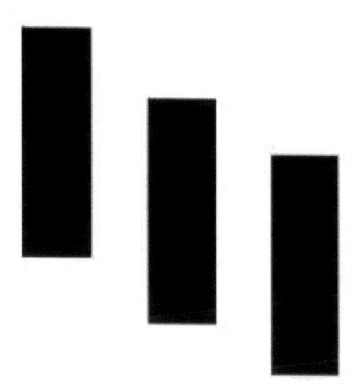

The *three black crows pattern* is formed when three consecutive bearish candlesticks appear following a previous upward trend. These are indications that a reversal of trend can be expected.

Three White Soldiers

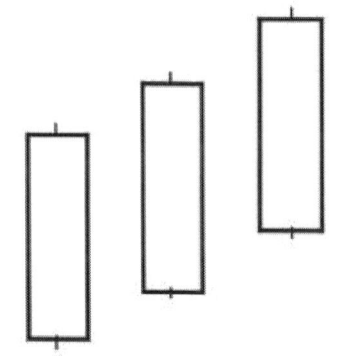

Three White Soldiers are the opposite of the three black crows. They usually appear following a strong downward trend, and suggest that a reversal of trend is occurring.

Key Lesson: These are just a sample of the many patterns that can appear in *candlestick charts*. There are many others and it would be useful to research and use these as you develop your trading skills. Often the trend patterns that have a higher degree of complexity using longer sequences of sequential *candlesticks* are more reliable.

Chapter 5: Technical Trading Techniques

5.1 Trends

You will probably have heard the phrase '*the trend is your friend*' and this is an extremely important message to remember. In order to utilise the various trading strategies discussed in this book, it is important to understand the market conditions that you are trading in. This will help to decide which tool you should apply in different circumstances. For example, *Fibonacci* can be applied easily to trending prices, whilst *pivot points* and *support/resistance levels* are best applied in a ranging market.

A *trending market* is one where prices are predominantly moving in one direction. There may be short term *retracements* during this period where prices move for a short period in a different direction, however, the general overall movement will remain on the same course. Alternatively, in a *ranging market* prices will fluctuate, moving both upwards and downwards with no clear pattern.

Key Lesson: There are often periods of price movement where there may be no discernable trend evident, and as a Forex beginner it is sometimes wise to try and avoid trading at these times. More experienced traders are able to find profits when prices are ranging and when there is only sideways movement in the market, but these periods can traditionally generate misleading signals and the volatility at these times can result in unpredictable swings in prices. As you gain more experience and understanding of strategies that can be employed in ranging conditions, then you can begin to take advantage of these opportunities as well.

Market conditions can be broken down into three main categories: *Upward trend*; *downward trend*; or *oscillating/ranging*.

5.1.1 Upward Trend

An *upward trend* develops when there are more buyers in the market active than sellers, thus, over the period, prices rise.

It is easy to recognise an *upward trend* when using technical analysis simply by connecting the lower troughs in the price movement. In an *upward trend*, when these are connected, they will form a clear upward sloping trend line, confirming the underlying movement.

Key Lesson: A general rule when drawing *trend lines* is that you should be able to connect at least three points on the line in order for it to be seen as a reliable indicator.

5.1.2 Downward Trend

Downward trends develop when there are more sellers of a particular currency than there are buyers, resulting in a drop in price over the period.

Technical analysis to identify a *downward trend* is achieved by connecting a series of progressively lower peaks or highs in the price movement. A minimum of three touching points is required to draw a reliable *downward trend line*.

5.1.3 Oscillation (Ranging)

When there is no clearly discernable trend evident in the price movements, then the price is said to be *oscillating or ranging*. During this period there are swings in price movement, often between levels of support and resistance, as the price bounces between the boundaries of a particular range.

5.1.4 Drawing Trend Lines

Trend lines are one of the simplest forms of technical analysis, and if used correctly can also be extremely effective. They should always be the first form of analysis used, and wherever possible combined with other technical analysis techniques in order to accurately plot the current market dynamics.

Drawing trend lines simple requires locating and then connecting two major tops or bottoms in price movement. Two points of contact are necessary to establish a trend, and then a third is required to confirm the trend. In an upward trend the line will connect the lower points of support (troughs), and in a downward trend the line will connect the upper point of resistance (peaks).

Drawing Trend Lines

There are three types of trend: Upwards, Downwards and Ranging (Sideways).

The steeper a trend, then the less reliable it is likely to be, and, therefore, the higher the chance of it being broken. The more points that can be connected along a line, the stronger the significance of the trend.

Key Lesson: It is important to always draw a trend line based upon the information available, and not to make the mistake of trying to fit the data to a perceived trend.

5.2 Support and Resistance

Support and Resistance are two concepts that are considered extremely important for technical analysis. The two can be sometimes difficult to understand as there are often different opinions, amongst traders, as to how best to calculate *support and resistance* levels.

There are often times, when prices are moving in a particular direction, where a level is reached beyond which traders will struggle to push prices. When this is seen in an upward price movement, then these levels are known as *resistance*. They act like a ceiling on prices, preventing movement beyond them. Conversely, when these levels are reached in a downward direction then they are known as *support*, and they act like a floor preventing prices from dropping lower.

These levels develop in response to activity in the market and as a result of overall market sentiment. If traders feel that a price is moving upwards too quickly or becoming overvalued then whenever any group of traders attempts to push prices higher than the resistance level, the majority of the market will resist this action. This means the market has decided that a price above that level would be too high and that they would be unwilling to pay those prices for that currency. Essentially, this lack of demand produces the *resistance*. The opposite is true in the case of *support* levels. This time, if the overriding market sentiment is that the price is falling below a value that the majority of traders feel it should be trading at, then there can be said to be *support*. This means that traders are generally supporting the current prices and feel that the value should not drop below current levels.

Often when the price hits one of these areas of *support or resistance*, it results in the price rebounding in the opposite direction. This can lead to either a significant reversal of movement, or just a temporary adjustment.

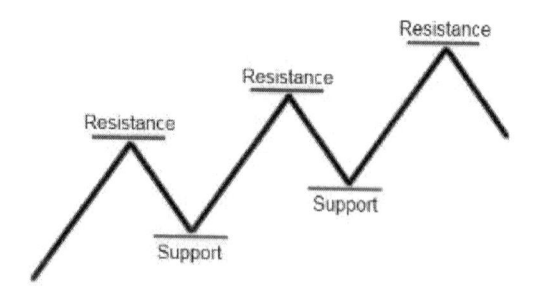

Although *support and resistance* levels do act as a boundaries of price movement, that is not to say that they are unbreakable. Often prices will range between particular levels of *support and resistance* for a period of time, as traders attempt to determine whether the price should be proceeding higher or lower. If an event should occur that begins to push prices predominately in one direction then it is much more likely that either the *support or resistance* level will be broken. Once the price succeeds in breaking through one of these levels, then new levels of *resistance and support* will develop, which factor these changes.

As a result of these changes *support and resistance* levels should be seen as dynamic entities, meaning they constantly readjust and move in relation to movements of prices.

There are numerous ways of calculating these *support and resistance* levels, many of which will be addressed in later sections.

Support & Resistance

Key Lesson: It is widely accepted that support and resistance levels are credible 'signposts' of areas where activity is likely to happen. This means that at these levels it is possible to expect, prices to either breakthrough, or rebound. It is possible to plan trades that can capitalise should either of these events occur.

5.3 Pivot Points

Pivot points are one method that can be used to calculate levels of *support* or *resistance*, which are crucial for indicating a change in price movement. They may be used to identify levels at which a price is likely to reverse, or values that prices must pass in order to signify specific price breakouts. Essentially, *pivot points* are used as important markers to anticipate when changes in price may occur, and as part of trading strategies to determine when and where transactions should be undertaken.

Pivot points are calculated in a number of ways, and generally this can be done automatically using charting software. It is important to have a basic grasp of the underlying methodology of generating *pivot points*. Outlined below is the most common calculation method, which is known as the *Five-Point System*:

Pivot Point = (High + Low + Close) / 3

First Support = (Pivot Point x 2) − High

First Resistance = (Pivot Point x 2) − Low

Second Support = Pivot Point − (High − Low)

Second Resistance = Pivot Point + (High − Low)

Charting software can be used to transpose these values as visual representations onto currency charts.

Pivot Points

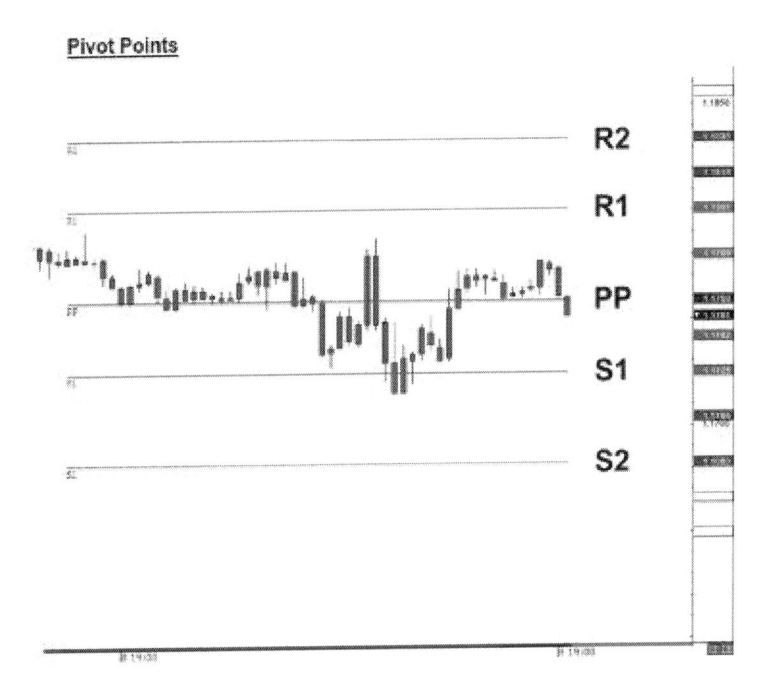

As the Forex market operates 24hrs a day the values for calculating these levels are usually taken at 4pm EST. Other methods of calculating *pivot points* can be used and it may be helpful to have some knowledge of these other methodologies.

5.3.1 Using Pivot Points

Pivot points are an extremely effective tool for intra-day trading, as they provide strong indications of levels of *support* and *resistance* within the market. The *pivot point* itself is the primary level of *support* or *resistance*, and it is at this point where the largest price movement can be expected to occur. In essence it can be expected that the price will either *'bounce off'* the *pivot point* or *'break through'* it.

Pivot Point - Bounce

Pivot points can be used to determine when trends are developing in the market. If the price breaks below the *pivot point* then this indicates the formation of a general downward trend, similarly when the price breaks above this level then it can suggest the start of an upward trend. Where prices bounce off the *pivot point* then this suggests a period of consolidation where there is no specific trend present.

Pivot Point - Breakthrough

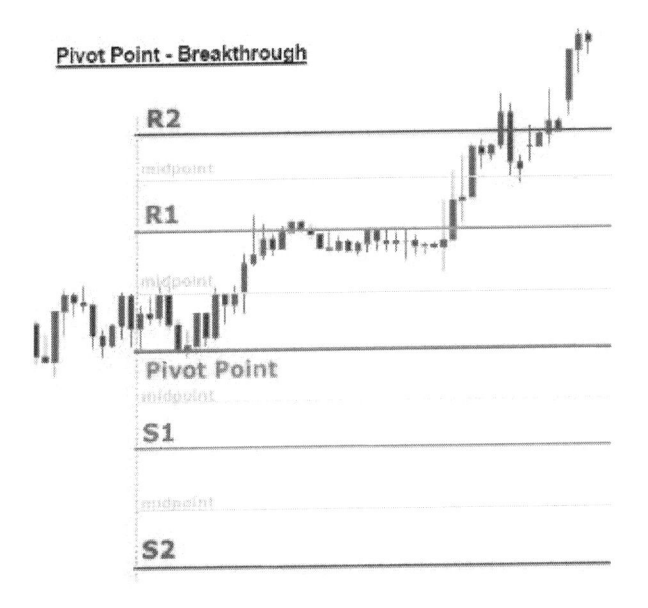

As *pivot points* are based upon the results of the previous day they are only a short-term indicator and need to be recalculated on a daily basis. This is done automatically by most charting software.

Pivot points can also be a very useful tool for determining when and where to enter and exit the market. The method for doing this relies upon the *pivot point* to signpost these entry and exit levels.

For example, if the price breaks below the *pivot point* you could use this as an indication to enter the market. You would then use the *pivot point* price to set a s*top loss* (ideally this should be placed just above this level in order to prevent your trade being closed early should the price rebound back towards the *pivot point* at any time). The *first support level* should then be used as the target price for that particular trade. If the price continues to move below this *first support level* then you could either choose to exit the trade, taking your profit, or, you could decide to reposition your *stop loss* using the *first support level* as its new position. In this case the profit target would now become the *second support level*.

By following this method and using *pivot points* to set the various *strategic levels* each trade should be well positioned to take advantage of the trending prices whilst remaining protected from any rebounds or reversals in movement.

There are some factors associated with the use of *pivot points* which necessitate a degree of caution. Often it is difficult to determine how the market is reacting at any given time, and if the price hovers around the *pivot point* then it can be hard to distinguish in which direction a future move may be. Occasionally prices will also reverse before actually reaching the set levels of support and resistance, resulting in a failed strategy.

Key Lesson: It is important to use *pivot points* in conjunction with other indicators, and to ensure that the overall market trend is taken into account when predicting possible movements. Trading against the trend should be avoided where possible!

5.4 Volume

In addition to monitoring price fluctuations another vital aspect of *technical analysis*, is being aware of the level of activity taking place in the marketplace at any given time, and this means understanding *volume*. *Volume* simply indicates the number of trades taking place over a period of time, providing useful information as to the number of traders currently active, as well as showing the market interest in buying or selling of a particular currency.

Most charting software will provide *volume* levels for preceding periods at the bottom of each chart. In just the same way that movements in the actual market price can reveal important information, so to trends can be determined via the analysis of *volume* levels.

There is actually no true measure of *volume* in the Forex markets owing to the scale and magnitude of the number of individual trades taking place daily, and the lack of centralised organisation to monitor this multitude of transactions. However, market makers will be aware of the approximate volumes of transactions occurring at any given time, and it is these figures which can be useful to track.

Each bar in a chart depicting *volume* will indicate the number of trades executed in that given period, as well as illustrating whether overall there was a greater net number of buy or sell orders.

It is important to remember to monitor *volume*, as it will often support the evidence for the accuracy of a particular trend. Where there is a price movement either up or down which is accompanied by a relatively high *volume* of trading activity, then it is more likely to be a reliable trend movement than if *volume* levels were significantly lower.

Key Lesson: Practically, this means that whenever you have identified a particular trend, by whatever means, then it is essential to check the *volume* levels to identify whether trading levels support your analysis.

Volume levels also generally move in accordance with the prevailing trend. Therefore, as a trend develops momentum in a particular direction this will often be accompanied by increasing *volume*, suggesting that there are an increasing number of market participants reinforcing the trend. This will ultimately help to push prices ever higher as traders move to take advantage of the rising or falling trend. As the support amongst traders for a particular trend begins to decrease then this will be accompanied by a relative drop in the levels of *volume*, as traders become wary of the underlying trend. This adoption of a more cautious position tends to signal either a period of consolidation or suggests that a trend reversal may be imminent.

As well as supporting the identification of underlying trends, *volume* can also be an important factor when using technical analysis chart patterns. In these instances *volume* becomes a factor, when particular patterns form, in determining whether the expected outcome of that pattern is likely to occur and whether the interpretation of market conditions is supported by other traders.

Chapter 6: Common Chart Patterns

Effective technical analysis requires the identification of patterns in charted information as well as an understanding of what these specific pattern formations indicate. Experienced traders will use chart patterns as a blueprint to develop individual trading strategy.

Knowing how the market is likely to react when any of these *chart patterns* appear allows traders to determine the buy and sell signals that signpost when and where to enter and exit trades.

Key Lesson: *Chart patterns* are usually good indicators of impending breakout movement. These provide the opportunities for good profit potential.

6.1 Continuation and Reversal Patterns

Most *chart patterns* develop and can be seen in price movement during periods of either *continuation* or *reversal*. The exact interpretation of each *chart pattern* is dependent upon a number of factors, but essentially they provide information as to whether a price is likely to continue heading in the direction of the prevailing trend (*continuation pattern*) or, if the price is set to have a reversal in trend and begin heading in the opposite direction to preceding movements (*reversal pattern*). A number of *chart patterns* will appear during periods of market consolidation and it is important to learn in each case whether the pattern suggests *continuation* or *reversal* of the price.

Key Lesson: *Chart patterns* are not an exact science and it is only by gaining experience over time that it becomes possible to learn to understand how, why and when they form. A trader can then begin to interpret the meaning of a patterns presence and ultimately how it may be used as a part of a profitable trading strategy.

6.2 Chart Patterns - Heads and Shoulders

Heads and shoulders is the term used to describe one of the most reliable chart patterns. This particular type of pattern can be categorised as a *reversal pattern*, which, when seen should suggest that the future price movement is likely to progress in the opposite direction to that of the preceding trend.

There are two main categories of this particular type of pattern. The *head and shoulder top* usually forms at the upper part of an upward trend and is a strong indication that the price is set to fall back. The opposite formation is that of the *head and shoulder bottom*, which may also be referred to as an *inverse head and shoulder*. In this case the pattern usually forms towards the bottom of a downward trend, and provides a significant indication of an imminent price reversal suggesting that the price will begin to rise against the earlier trend.

Both *head and shoulder* chart patterns develop as a sequence of four significant parts. The presence of all parts in succession represents an extremely reliable indication that the currency movement could be set for a reversal.

A true *head and shoulder* pattern will consist of an initial peak (*shoulder*) followed by a higher peak (*head*) and then subsequently another lower peak (*second shoulder*). The final element consists of a neckline which you should be able to create by drawing a line between the two troughs of the pattern. This neckline can be used as a critical level of support.

During the occurrence of a *head and shoulder* formation the price of the security should follow a specific pattern, which upon completion should result in the price reversal.

Head & Shoulder Top

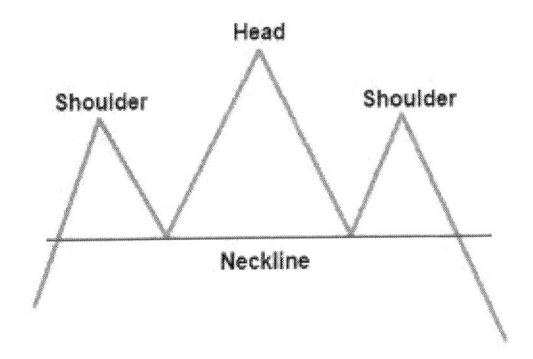

[Diagram showing a Head & Shoulder Top pattern with labels: Shoulder (left), Head (center, higher), Shoulder (right), and Neckline across the bottom]

The first *shoulder* is formed as the price rises to a new high for the period before peaking and experiencing a fall back. This short period of retreat is then followed by the price beginning to climb higher again reaching an overall high for the period. This occurs as traders attempt to test the markets' 'appetite' for a higher price level. If there is a lack of positive response to this test then the price will retreat again, forming the second higher peak or *head* element of the pattern. This price retreat will generally fall to a low similar to that seen in the first *shoulder*. The *second shoulder* of the pattern occurs when the price rises again, peaking at a level lower than that of the preceding *head* but at a level similar to, or slightly lower than that of the *first shoulder*. This happens as traders attempt once more to test the demand for higher prices. When this test fails and prices begin to fall below the *neckline* then this signifies the completion of the *head and shoulder pattern*.

The pattern provides a graphical illustration of events in the market highlighting a succession of failed attempts to push prices higher. These failures confirm a falling demand amongst traders, resulting in a reversal of the underlying trend.

Key Lesson: It is important to also consider and monitor volume levels whilst observing the formation of the *head and shoulder* pattern. A high increase in trading volume, corresponding with the prices movement through the neckline, provides additional evidence that the expected reversal is gaining momentum.

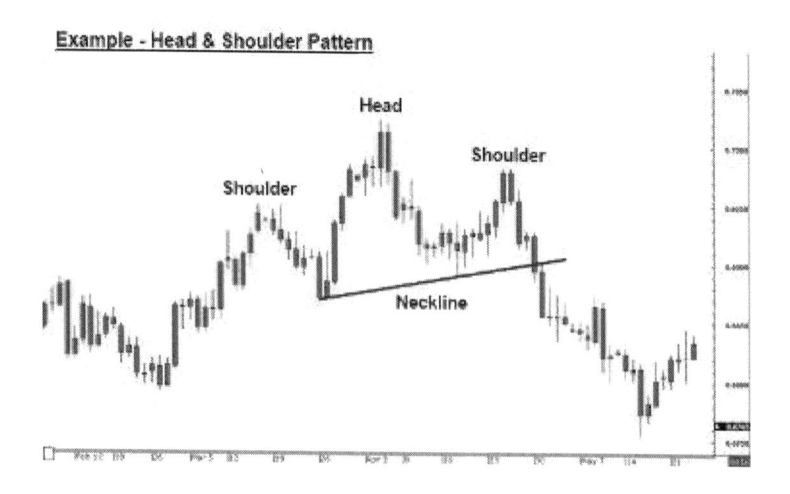

Example - Head & Shoulder Pattern

Trading Strategy: The breakout indication produced by the *head and shoulder* pattern, as we have seen, happens as the currency price passes through the *neckline*, therefore a good trading strategy will depend upon entering the market at the point of breakout or as the security passes the *neckline*.

A good rule-of-thumb when setting your profit target for a trade made in these circumstances is to measure the distance between the *head* and the *neckline*, and to use this same measure (applied from the *neckline*, in the new direction) as a target price.

Often, the trend should continue in this new direction as expected, but it is important to be aware that *fall-back* may occur. This is where the price briefly breaks past the neckline but then retreats back above or below it. Often this occurs as the market tests the levels of support and resistance related to the new trend. This activity can actually strengthen the significance of the pattern and when the price moves again in the direction of the new trend you can rely upon this movement to a greater extent.

6.2.1 Inverse/Bottom Head and Shoulder

In the case of an *inverse* or *bottom head and shoulder* then the same formations can be expected to occur, but in the opposite direction.

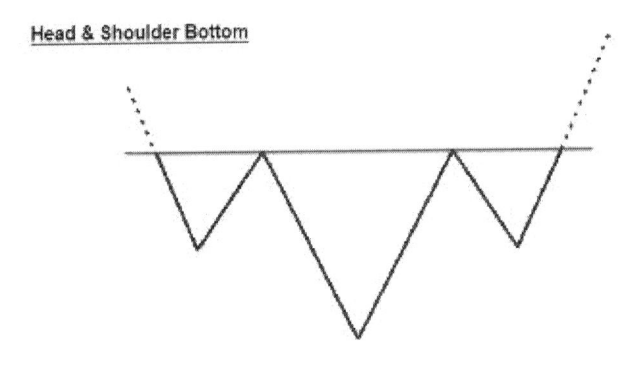

Head & Shoulder Bottom

6.3 Triangles

There are a number of chart patterns which use different types of triangle formations to identify potential opportunities in the market.

6.3.1 Symmetrical Triangles

Symmetrical triangles can either represent a period of consolidation or a period of indecision amongst market participants. Typically, during this time supply and demand are at fairly equal levels.

Key Lesson: *Symmetrical triangles* can be an essential indicator to help decide when to enter the market. This pattern often leads to a continuation of the prior trend. For example, where the preceding trend was downward, then it is reasonable to expect a downwards break below the ascending support line as the price nears the apex of the triangle. Conversely, if the preceding trend had been upward then the break is likely to be in an upward direction moving above the descending resistance line and continuing the trend. There are times however, when this pattern does not always follow the prevailing trend and it is important to be prepared for *false breakouts*.

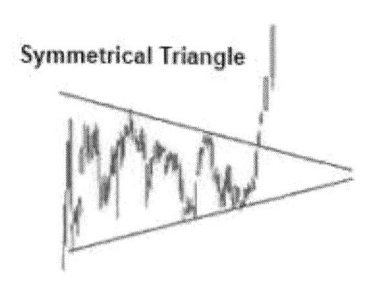

Symmetrical Triangle

The triangle is formed by the convergence of a descending resistance line and an ascending support line. These lines should have a similar slope and will converge at a common apex. Within the pattern each new peak and trough, formed by lower tops and higher bottoms, will become closer following the shape of the *triangle*. Lower volumes usually accompany this period. The price will continue to bounce between these trend-lines, as it nears the apex, before finally breaking out.

The underlying cause for this particular pattern is that it represents a phase when traders are 'indecisive' as to where the price is likely to go in the near future. This produces a period where prices can be said to be in *consolidation*, also sometimes described as *sideways movement*. As the *symmetrical triangle* pattern forms it suggests the number of buyers and sellers are in relative equilibrium for a short period of time. As the price nears the apex of the triangle then this period of consolidation completes with prices moving in a clear breakout-often in the direction of the preceding trend.

Trading Strategy: Once a *symmetrical triangle* pattern has been identified, it is possible to use it to determine trading entry points. By placing entry orders just above the descending line of resistance, and just below the ascending line of support it is possible to capitalise on any forthcoming breakout. Although you should be expecting a breakout in the direction of the preceding trend, this strategy covers you should the opposite occur. When the breakout begins and the entry order is hit, then the opposite entry order can be cancelled. Prudent placement of *stop-losses* can then be used to lock-in any profitable gains.

6.3.2 Ascending Triangles

Ascending triangles will generally be constructed with a flat top, formed by a line of resistance, and an upward sloping bottom formed by a line of support - created by a period of increasingly higher lows.

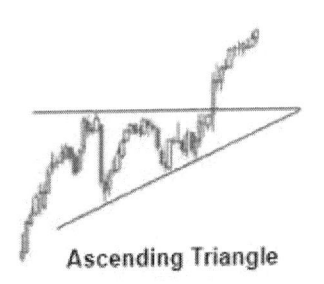

Ascending Triangle

The pattern typically represents periods of continuation and is commonly seen as an indication of bullish market activity. As such *ascending triangles* are most reliable when found as part of an upward trend. In a similar manner to a *symmetrical triangle* prices should move up and down between the two lines of support and resistance prior to breaking out to the upper-side of the resistance line. *Ascending triangles* can at times also be found in a downward bearish trend, but, in these circumstances, the pattern is of less significance.

Key Lesson: The price will bounce between the two lines, as buyers struggle to push prices higher in order to break the current resistance level. The presence of the increasingly higher lows at the support level indicates that there are gradually fewer sellers, which eventually allows buyers to push the price beyond the level of resistance, leading to a continuation of the trend.

Trading Strategy: As has been seen, the *ascending triangle* pattern is completed when the price breaks above the resistance line and it is this indication that should be used to plan tradable entry points. In some cases, the trend may not continue as predicted and the price may fall back below the support line. It is, therefore, sensible to ensure that a genuine breakout is occurring in the correct upward direction, before entering a trade.

6.3.3 Descending Triangles

Descending triangle patterns work in the opposite manner to that of *ascending triangles*, and as such are usually used as an indication of a bearish market. The *descending triangle* pattern is formed from a flat bottom support line and a downward-sloping resistance line.

Descending Triangle

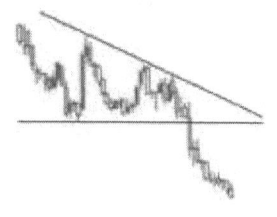

Prices should again bounce between the two lines, but this time the indication taken from the existence of the pattern would be that ultimately the price will descend below the existing support line, and continue in a downward trend. When the pattern is seen in a period where the preceding trend has been in a downward direction, then it can be more reliably expected that any breakout will also occur in that same direction.

In a similar manner to *ascending triangles* it is necessary to be aware that the breakout may also happen in the reverse direction and so caution should be taken when planning transactions to prepare for this eventuality.

6.4 Flags and Pennants

Flags and *pennants* are continuation patterns that usually follow strong price movements. They most often occur during periods of price consolidation following dynamic market activity. When the price movements for a period create a rectangle pattern then this is known as a *flag* whereas when the pattern forms a triangle it is known as a *pennant*.

When a price moves strongly upwards or downwards, there are often periods during which traders 'pause' and prices consolidate before activity begins again and traders once more seek to push prices either higher or lower, depending upon whether the prevailing trend was upward or downwards. *Flag* and *pennant* patterns are formed during these periods and will often provide a good indication that can be used to prepare for imminent breakouts.

6.4.1 Flags

Flags are reliable patterns that are generally found after a large price movement in a particular direction. A rectangle shape created by temporary support and resistance lines form the basis for the *flag*, which will generally slope in a direction away from the preceding price movement. This should be accompanied by a simultaneous reduction in trade volumes.

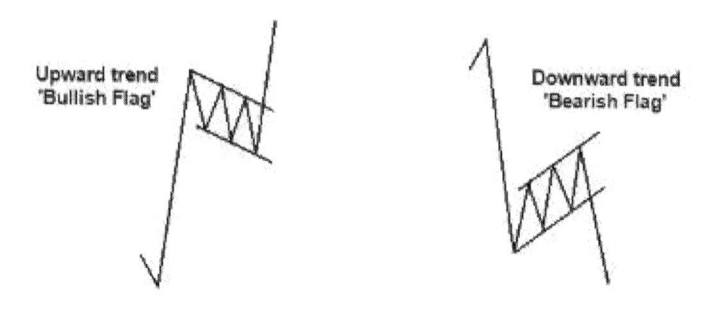

Upward trend 'Bullish Flag'

Downward trend 'Bearish Flag'

The occurrence of this pattern accompanied by a reduction in market activity represents a period of consolidation where prices over the short term back-track. During this time traders evaluate the significance of the preceding large price movement and there will be a degree of profit taking. The completion of the *flag* pattern will suggest that there is sufficient appetite amongst traders to continue the preceding trend.

Trading Strategy: Once the price breaks through the temporary support or resistance lines then it becomes a strong indication of continued price movement, and this can be used to plan transactions that take advantage of that movement. Higher volume levels will often accompany any breakout so where these two events occur, the validity of the pattern is strengthened.

6.4.2 Pennants

Pennants work in a similar manner to *flags* and can provide equally effective trading indications. They follow a triangular pattern similar to that of *symmetrical triangles* where temporary lines of support and resistance are used to produce the upper and lower limbs of the *pennant* which, over time, will converge at a common apex. *Pennants* whilst similar in pattern to *flags* will often form in a flatter horizontal configuration.

As with *flags* the expectation with a *pennant* pattern is that the price will (following a brief period of consolidation during which appetite amongst traders for additional price movement is assessed) breakout in the same direction as the prior trend.

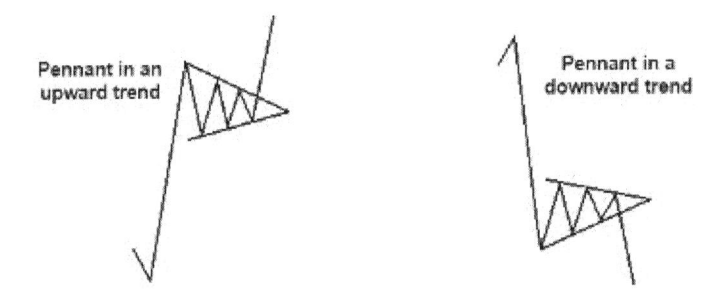

Pennant in an upward trend

Pennant in a downward trend

Trading Strategy: *Flags* and *pennants* can both be utilised as effective and significant trade signals. Where there is an upward trend a buy order should be placed just above the upper limb of the *flag* or *pennant* and a stop loss placed just below (to prevent losses should a breakout prove false). In a downward trend then the opposite of this method should be followed.

Key Lesson: *Flags* and *pennants* are commonly used amongst traders as they are both reliable continuation patterns which tend to only rarely result in an unexpected reversal of trend.

6.5 Wedges

The *wedge* chart pattern tends to form over longer periods of time compared to other patterns, often taking between 2-6 months to fully develop. The pattern can represent both periods of continuation or reversal, and forms in a similar manner and shape to that of the *symmetrical triangle* pattern.

The pattern will generally develop as either a *rising wedge* or a *descending wedge*. It can be difficult to accurately determine whether the pattern will result in continuation or reversal but the general rule follows that a *rising wedge* should indicate conditions for a bearish market whereas a *descending wedge* should indicate that current conditions suggest a bullish market.

6.5.1 Rising Wedges

A *rising wedge* forms when prices begin to consolidate, enclosed between the upward sloping lines of support and resistance. The line of support will usually be steeper than that of the line of resistance, suggesting that *higher lows* are being formed more quickly than the *higher highs*. This creates a period of sideways movement which forms a distinctive *wedge* shape. As we have seen previously, patterns which illustrate periods of price consolidation tend to predict significant forthcoming price action and this is also the case with *wedge patterns*. As the pattern forms, it is fair to expect some significant price movement in the foreseeable future.

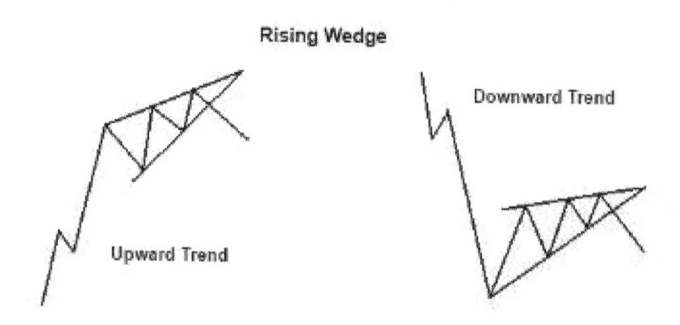

Rising Wedge

When a *rising wedge* forms following a preceding upward trend, then it will often suggest that a future price reversal could be expected. Whereas, when the pattern appears as part of a preceding downward trend, then it often tends to indicate that there is likely to be a further continuation of that downward trend.

6.5.2 Falling Wedges

In a similar manner to the *rising wedge*, the *falling wedge* pattern can also signify either the continuation, or reversal of a trend. When a *falling wedge* pattern is observed towards the bottom of a downward trend, then this can often suggest that the market is preparing for a price reversal. Alternatively, when a *falling wedge* is found in a period with an upward trend, then it tends to signify a period of consolidation, where, upon completion of the full pattern, prices could be predicted to move in a continuation of the preceding trend.

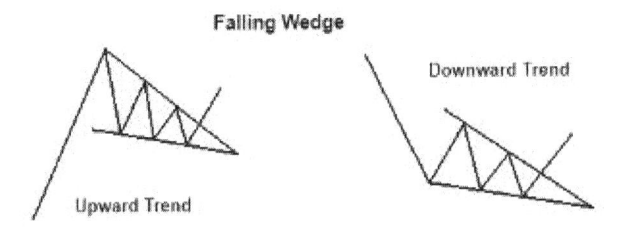

Falling Wedge

Upward Trend

Downward Trend

Key Lesson: A *rising wedge* can be considered as a *bearish* pattern which will result in downward price movement. This means that, when it is observed in an upward trend, it will, in most cases, result in a reversal and subsequent downward movement, whereas, when it is seen in a downward trend it should result in the continuation of that downward trend.

By contrast, the *falling wedge* should be viewed as a *bullish* chart pattern, meaning that it should generally lead to upward price movement.

6.6 Rectangles

Rectangle chart patterns are found when the price becomes bounded by parallel lines of support and resistance, as a result of the price oscillating between fairly regular levels of highs and lows. Formation of the pattern often suggests that the market is in a period of consolidation, or that there is currently substantial indecision amongst traders as to where future prices are heading. This phase of price rebound will mean that both the levels of support and resistance are being periodically tested by buyers and sellers, to determine in which direction a breakout may occur. The critical point with *rectangles* is that the breakout could occur in either direction.

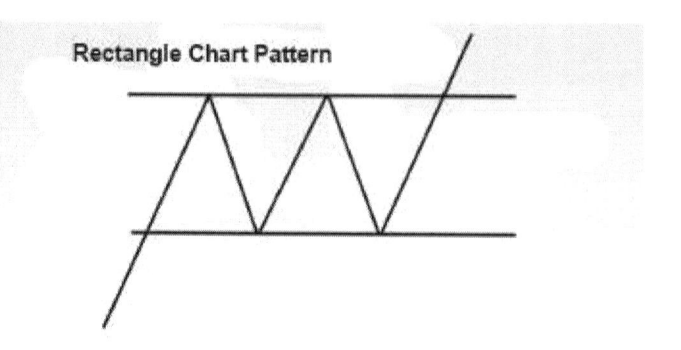

Rectangle Chart Pattern

Often price movement may follow the direction of a preceding trend however, this should not be taken for granted. The main point to remember is that when the breakout does occur, it should result in fairly dynamic price activity. Either way, the point of breakout can be employed to determine potential trading entry points, so as to take full advantage of the new trend.

Key Lesson: Once the direction of the breakout has been identified and a trade entered, then a potential target price can be determined by taking a measure of the rectangle and using this as a guide for the price movement below or above the broken level of support or resistance.

Example - Rectangle Chart Pattern

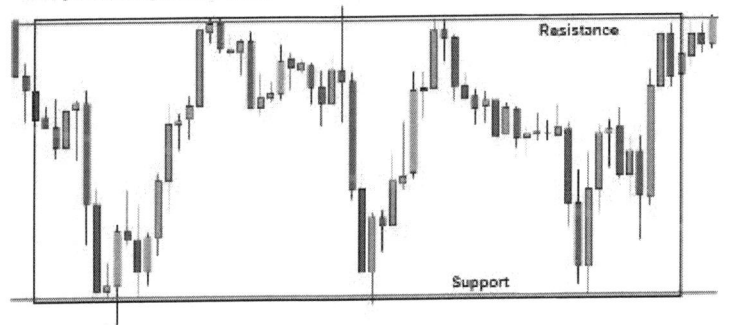

6.7 Double Top and Double Bottom

The *double top* and *double bottom* chart patterns both tend to be reversal patterns which, when seen should strongly suggest that the currency price in the near future is set to begin moving in the opposite direction.

Double Top Chart Pattern

In a *double top* pattern the price will twice try to push higher than a particular level and when it fails to do so over two successive attempts, then the trend often reverses resulting in the price moving lower. Where the second *top* of the *double top* is slightly lower than the first, then this can further support the likelihood of a reversal occurring. The opposite can be said to happen in the case of a *double bottom*.

The *double top* or *double bottom* patterns often form following the strong movement of a preceding trend. They develop when the price on two occasions attempts to break through the same level of either support, or resistance and fails to do so at each attempt. By rebounding from the level of support or resistance, this type of price movement illustrates that traders are trying to test whether there is sufficient appetite to push the price through that particular level. Failure to do so on two successive occasions usually signifies that there is a lack of demand for higher/lower prices in the marketplace, which will often be sufficient to drive the price into reversal and mark the beginning of a new trend.

Key Lesson: A *double top* is most likely to occur at the top of a strong upward trend, and when both are seen together then the indication of the pattern becomes more reliable. The same connection can be observed between a strong downward trend and the *double bottom* pattern.

Trading Strategy: By drawing a neckline linking the bases of the two peaks formed in a *double top*, this can be used to position your entry orders. By placing the order just below this level, it becomes possible to capitalise on a breakout if it occurs as predicted. The drop in price below the neckline will often correspond to the height of the *double top* peaks from the neckline, and this can be used as a useful measure when setting a profit target. The same method can be employed, just in the opposite direction, when dealing with a *double bottom*.

In some cases, price movements may actually test the support or resistance levels on three separate occasions, and, in these circumstances, the pattern can be described as a *triple top* or *triple bottom*.

6.8 Round Bottoms and Tops

A *round bottom* is a long term chart pattern that can occur over a few months or over a number of years. It is a reversal pattern that forms as a steady curved trough indicating the long-term transition from a downward trend to an upward trend. This type of pattern will often occur in conjunction with improving fundamental evidence that would suggest a currency is gradually improving in strength and quality. The opposite can also be found when an upward trend gradually transforms to a downward trend whereby the pattern created is referred to as a *rounded top*.

6.9 Chart Patterns - Conclusions

As we have seen *chart patterns* are an extremely useful part of any currency trader's toolbox. Whilst it may seem that spotting them can prove a difficult task, by taking the time and patience to thoroughly learn and observe when and how these patterns are likely to occur, they should gradually become a vital element of everyday technical analysis. Over time these skills will allow you to more accurately determine current market conditions and to make appropriate decisions as to what could happen in the future.

Key Lesson: Outlined below is a brief summary recapping the different *chart patterns* and highlighting whether they fall into the three categories of *continuation patterns*, *reversal patterns,* or *binary patterns*:

Continuation Patterns

The presence of a *continuation pattern* suggests that prices will continue to follow the direction of the preceding trend.

- Rising Wedge
- Falling Wedge
- Bullish Rectangle

- Bearish Rectangle
- Bullish Flag/Pennant
- Bearish Flag/Pennant

Reversal Patterns

A *reversal pattern* signals that there is likely to be a change in the direction of price movement away from the preceding trend.

- Head and Shoulders
- Inverse Head and Shoulders
- Rising Wedge
- Falling Wedge
- Double Top
- Double Bottom

Binary Patterns

A *binary pattern* represents a period of consolidation, after which the market may respond, by driving prices in *either* direction. This could mean continuation of the preceding trends or lead to a reversal of that trend. Only once the pattern has been completed and a breakout occurs can the new trend be identified.

- Symmetrical Triangle
- Ascending Triangle
- Descending Triangle

Chapter 7: Moving Averages

The term *moving average* refers to a method of analysis that can be used to smooth out the fluctuations in price movement over a given period of time, so as to provide a clear uncomplicated representation of the currency movements during that period.

When a currency pair is illustrated using a normal chart that plots all the oscillations in price movement, the level of detail can sometimes mean that it is difficult to see when an underlying trend is forming or to identify opportunities for trading. *Moving averages* help to reduce these fluctuations by plotting only average values, resulting in a much smoother charted representation. These can be more easily read and help to understand the movement that is occurring over the period, ultimately making it easier to spot any core trends.

Key Lesson: A *moving average* is calculated by using the average closing prices for a currency pair over the previous 'x' number of periods.

There are different types of *moving average* which can be employed. The more prices are averaged, over longer periods of time, then the smoother the resulting trend line that is produced. Generally, the smoother the *moving average* (the longer time frame over which it has been averaged) then the slower it is to react to short term price fluctuations. Conversely, the more rugged the trend line of a moving average (one averaged out over fewer time periods) then the closer it will track short-term changes in price.

Moving averages are a *lagging indicator*, which means they do not primarily predict new trends but serve to confirm and support the identification of trends once they have been established.

There are two main classes of *moving average*: *Simple* and *exponential*.

7.1 Simple Moving Average (SMA)

Simple moving averages are, as the name suggests, the simplest type of *moving average* to calculate. Whereby you would simply add 'x' number of closing prices together and then divide by 'x'. The value of 'x' will depend upon the number of time periods over which you wish to average the price.

Key Lesson: Should you wish to calculate a *ten period moving average* on a one-minute chart, then you would take the closing prices for each of the last ten one-minute periods, add them all together and divide by the total number of periods, which in this case would be ten. When using charting software, then the *moving average* will be represented by a line and drawn on the chart accordingly. Charting software will often abbreviate any labels applied to read in the following format - *10 SMA*. The number simply refers to the periods over which the *moving average* has been calculated.

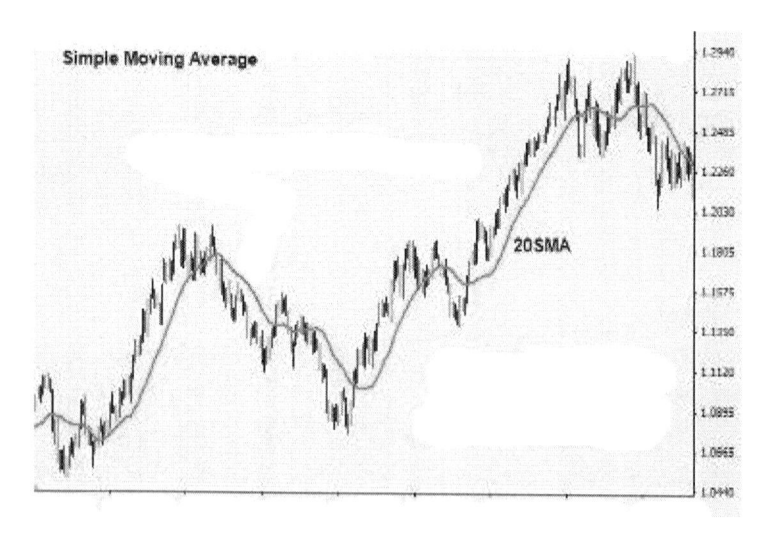

Whilst most charting software will calculate *moving averages* on your behalf and plot them accordingly as overlays on your currency charts, it is important to understand the underlying method by which they are calculated, in order to appreciate how they can be used effectively as a part of daily technical analysis. Knowledge of the *moving average* indicator and how it works makes it easier to adjust and personalise its component elements in order to fit with individual trading strategies. Charting software will allow you to adjust and edit the specific criteria of any *moving average* you use, depending upon your own specifications, so it is crucial to know how the figures used will affect the indicator and ultimately what the results will actually show.

The *simple moving average* provides a retrospective viewpoint, owing to the fact that it is calculated and based on past figures and from events that have already taken place. It, therefore, should not be interpreted as an 'all seeing' predictor of future events. However, it is extremely effective at highlighting emerging trends and can provide very useful signposts that relate to possible future price movements. Experienced traders will use *moving averages* in combination with other indicators and technical analysis techniques in order to help them gain a greater understanding of market conditions and identify potential trading opportunities.

Whilst *simple moving averages* are very useful as a means of viewing the broader market conditions, they can, at times, be obscured by rapid fluctuations or spikes in prices. If there is a sudden price movement that only results in temporary price peaks, then this can distort the accuracy of the *moving average*, especially over shorter periods of time. This in turn can result in the identification of false trends. It is, therefore important to always monitor *actual price movements* in conjunction with any *moving average* indicators.

7.2 Exponential Moving Average (EMA)

The *exponential moving average indicator* helps to reduce some of the problems that can occur with *simple moving averages*. This time the calculation is adjusted in order to reduce the effect that temporary *price spikes* may have on the accuracy of the indicator.

The calculation of *exponential moving averages* does this by placing more emphasis on the price values of recent time periods and less on those that are further in the past. This manipulation of the figures helps to produce a more accurate illustration of the trading activity happening in the short-term. Ultimately, this provides a better overall picture of current market conditions.

As a result, *exponential moving averages* (*EMA's*) are much more responsive to the influences of new information than their *SMA* counterparts. Traders generally tend to prefer *EMA's* specifically because of this greater level of response.

7.3 Using Moving Averages

Moving averages are an effective indicator of the current market conditions and should be used regularly as a component of your technical analysis to discover underlying price trends and to reveal trading opportunities.

Where a *moving average* is heading in an upward direction and is below the actual price value, then this should signal that there is a prevailing upward trend. When the *moving average* is heading in a downward direction but remains above the current currency price value, then this suggests the presence of a downward trend.

Whilst the above statements are both true, in reality it is not always so straight forward to practically use such determinations. If you are only using one particular *moving average,* then it can be susceptible to providing *false indications* and unreliable breakout signals. A *false indication*, for example, may occur when an unexpected news item or event causes short-term reaction amongst market participants, resulting in price movements in the opposite direction to the prevailing trend. In many cases, a reaction like this will be short lived, meaning that once the market has digested the news story or event, prices tend to revert back to the earlier trend. Because the moving average takes longer to react to the event, the line representing it on a chart can end up on the wrong side, above or below, of the line being used to plot the actual current price. In this case, if you were to follow the axiom mentioned earlier, then it would suggest that a reversal of trend could be occurring. However, in these circumstances that assumption would be wrong. The price movement only briefly reacted to the news before continuing with the prevailing trend, meaning that the signal was *false*.

To avoid any false signals and confusion, most traders will often use more than one *moving average* at any one time in order to increase the reliability of the indication they provide.

Key Lesson: For example, plotting two *moving averages* on a chart will provide a much clearer and more reliable indication of when the price is trending up or down than if you were to solely rely upon just one. To do this, it is necessary to plot two *moving averages* with sufficiently different time periods as this will help to provide a clearer picture of market conditions. When a *faster moving average* (10 SMA) and a *slower moving average* (20 SMA) are simultaneously plotted on a chart then generally, when the faster MA is above the slower MA it will indicate that the price is in an upward trend. In a downward, trend then the faster MA should be below the slower MA.

7.4 Moving Averages to Determine Momentum

Any successful trading strategy requires a method to gauge *price momentum* (relative strength of any movement) in order to help identify potential market movement and ultimately determine profitable trading events. *Moving averages* are seen by many as an extremely effective measure of this market *momentum*. The technique of using *moving averages MAs* to determine this *momentum* is to apply and utilise multiple *MAs* that have been calculated using different time frames. In general, *short-term momentum* can be identified using *MAs* with a time period of 20 days or less; *medium-term momentum* can be gauged with *MAs* of 20-100 days; and *longer-term momentum* can be seen using *MAs* with periods of greater than 100 days.

In practice, many Forex trades will be conducted over much shorter periods than this, however the same principles apply.

A good measure of overall *price momentum* is to plot three different moving averages on a chart, each with a different time period, ideally representing the *long-term momentum* (longer time period), *medium-term momentum* and *short-term momentum*. The interaction between this combination of *MAs* will help to give a clear signal as to whether the market is in an upward, or downward, phase as well as providing a measure of the relative strength of that price movement.

When the short-term *MA* is located above the other longer-term *MAs* on the chart, then this will often indicate a bullish upward trend present in the market, especially when the short-term MA is diverging upwards and away from the other two. When the short-term *MA* is below the other two longer-term indicators and is diverging downwards, then this should provide strong indications that there is a bearish downward trend prevailing.

7.5 Moving Average Crossovers

Traders use the interactions between *long and short-term MAs* in order to determine **buy** and **sell** signals. When a *short-term MA* crosses above a *longer-term MA,* also known as a *Bullish Crossover,* it generally suggests growing momentum within the marketplace. It also highlights that prices in the short term are rising at a faster rate than they have done over the longer period. Overall, the indication is used by traders as a **buy** signal. Conversely, when a *short-term MA* passes below a *longer-term MA* then this is known as a *Bearish Crossover*. In this circumstance traders will use the crossover as an indication that there is falling momentum and that short term prices are reducing in relation to longer term prices. This will generally be employed as a **sell** signal.

7.6 Moving Averages – Support and Resistance

Moving Averages can also be used as dynamic levels of support and resistance that adapt depending upon the current price movement.

Chapter 8: Indicators and Oscillators

The key to all technical analysis is to try and identify trends in price movements as they happen. There are many tools available to a trader which can help to achieve this. These tools tend to fall into two distinct categories of *indicators* and *oscillators*. They provide useful information relating to where trends are occurring, how they are developing, and suggest how the market may react to these movements in the near future.

As a trader, knowledge of these tools will help you to more easily and accurately identify potential trends and to uncover signals that will determine when, and where, to enter and exit the market with each trade.

Trading success requires a good working knowledge of all these tools, in addition to an understanding of how they are calculated, charted, and what they ultimately mean. Trading strategies will often use combinations of different *indicators* and *oscillators* to try to increase reliability.

8.1 Leading v. Lagging Indicators

There are two main types of *indicator*: *Leading indicators* (also known as *oscillating indicators* or simply *oscillators*) or *lagging indicators* (also known as *trending* or *momentum indicators*). *Lagging indicators* use price information in order to determine trends **after** they have begun, whereas *leading indicators* use the same information to attempt to determine trends in price movements **before** they have begun.

The main difference between the two types of *indicator* is related to the reliability of the results they produce. If it were possible to use leading indicators accurately all the time, then they would essentially be the 'holy grail' of Forex trading. It would be possible to foresee new trends before they begin and to profit from the predicted movements each and every time. However, unfortunately this is not how things work in real life. In reality, *leading indicators*, whilst extremely useful, are also notoriously difficult to interpret accurately and are regularly prone to providing unreliable indications. They will often predict *breakouts* which either fail to actually occur, or which do not produce any significant change in price. Despite this, *leading indicators* are still a vital element of any trader's toolbox, because when combined with other elements such as *fundamental analysis*, or when used in conjunction with supporting *lagging indicators*, they make it possible to predict when and how prices may change.

Lagging indicators, which are retrospective by nature, are considerably more reliable as they rely upon information and events that have already occurred as a means of revealing underlying trends. This does mean, however, that they can only be used to identify trending phases after they have begun, which means that it could be potentially too late to be able to profit from them.

8.2 Leading and Lagging Indicators - Summary

Key Lesson: The most important thing to remember, when it comes to using *indicators* of any type, is that they can only tell you either what the market has been doing, or what the market may do in the future, based upon analysis of the historic movement of the currency.

All *indicators* have been developed to interpret price information in slightly different ways and, therefore, they react differently to certain conditions. They are also developed under the assumption that the market will always have the same response to particular behaviour within the price movement, and this is simply not the case.

Trading Strategy: In order to successfully identify potential trends and future price activity it is vital to use a variety of both *lagging* and *leading indicators*. When this combination of *indicators* produces conflicting signals relating to where the market may be heading, then you should avoid making a trade.

Only trade when all the criteria of your individual trading strategy are present and when all your different *indicators* and sources of information reinforce each other.

8.3 Bollinger Bands

Bollinger bands are a form of technical analysis produced using the values of two standard deviations away from a particular *moving average*. It doesn't matter which *MA* is used, but by charting the two lines derived, using the standard deviations, it creates an *upper* and *lower band* to the top and bottom sides of the *MA*, which will track the price movement.

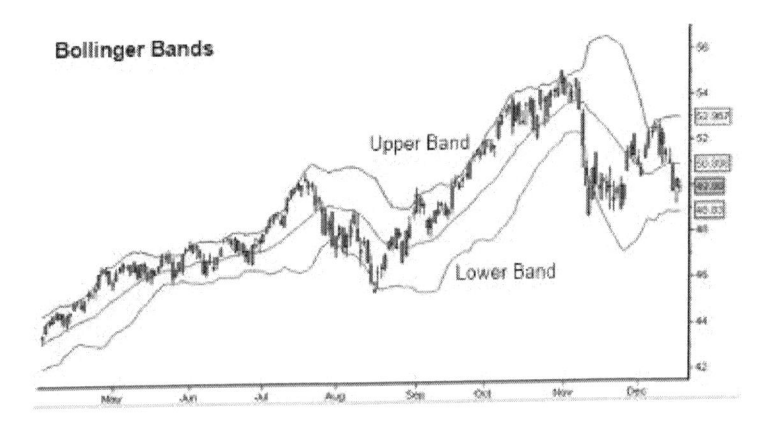

Whilst this description may sound complicated, in reality, all the necessary required calculations are performed by your charting software and the *bands* are plotted automatically. It is sufficient to have only a basic knowledge of how the figures are derived, what is more important is having an understanding how these *bands* can be effectively used.

Bollinger bands primarily provide a strong indication of market volatility. When the market becomes more volatile, the *bands* will **widen** and move away from the *MA* and when there is less volatility, the bands will **tighten** towards the *MA*.

The relationship between the *MA* and the *Bollinger bands* can also provide information relating to whether the currency is becoming *over-bought* or *over-sold* at any given time. As the actual currency price approaches the *upper band* then this will suggest that the currency is becoming *over-bought*. Conversely, when the price moves towards the *lower band* then it suggests that the currency is becoming *over-sold*.

Key Lesson: *Bollinger bands* are extremely useful as they indicate the relative levels of volatility in prices and, as such, provide a good measure of market conditions.

Trading Strategy: As well as being an extremely important indicator, *Bollinger bands* can also provide useful trading signals. The first thing to be aware of is that the price should tend to migrate towards the centre of the enclosing *Bollinger bands*. Knowing this, when the price does start to approach one or other of the *bands*, then it is likely that, if it hits them, it should subsequently rebound back towards the centre. This occurs because the *bands* act like dynamic levels of *support* and *resistance*. This pattern of rebounding is especially evident when there is no clear trend and the price ranges between these two levels. The longer the time frame used, then the more reliable *Bollinger bands* tend to be.

When there is a trend then *Bollinger bands* can also be used. As the *bands* begin to close together, this is usually a good indication of an imminent price breakout. When the price breaks through the *upper band*, then this will often signify the start of an upward price trend, and similarly, when the price breaks below the *lower band*, then this suggests a downward movement in price.

8.4 Moving Average – Convergence and Divergence (MACD)

The term *Moving Average Convergence and Divergence* often referred to by the acronym *MACD* is one of the most commonly used indicators amongst Forex traders. Whilst the name seems to suggest a potentially complicated analysis process, *MACD* is actually a relatively simple tool, that when used effectively, can determine short term price momentum.

To appreciate how the *MACD* tool can be implemented, it is important to fully understand the relationship between *long and short-term moving averages*. As discussed previously, traders will consider the interactions between *long and short-term MAs* in order to determine **buy** and **sell** signals. When a *short-term MA* crosses above a *longer-term MA*, also known as a *Bullish Crossover*, it generally suggests growing momentum within the marketplace. It also highlights that prices in the short term are rising at a faster rate than they have done over the longer period. Overall, the indication is used by traders as a **buy** signal. Conversely, when a *short-term MA* passes below a *longer-term MA* then this is known as a *Bearish Crossover*. In this circumstance traders will use the crossover as an indication that there is falling momentum and that short term prices are reducing in relation to longer term prices. This will generally be employed as a **sell** signal.

The *MACD* indicator utilises this relationship between *MAs* by analysing the *convergences* and *divergences*. In practice, this is achieved by subtracting the value of the long-term *MA* from that of the short-term *MA* and visually representing the results on a chart. The time periods of the component *MAs* can be adjusted to fit with individual trading strategy, however, generally the default periods will be sufficient.

Most charting software will present *MACD* data in the form of a histogram to make it easier to read and understand.

Key Lesson: When the *MACD* tool produces a positive value (a result of the short-term *MA* performing above the long-term counterpart), then this indicates that there is increasing upward momentum suggesting a good time to buy. Alternatively, when the opposite is true and the *MACD* produces a negative value, then this suggests falling momentum and should be used as a potential sell signal.

Trading Strategy: An effective method of using *MACD* in order to provide strong buy and sell transaction signals, is to combine the *MACD* plot with that of another *moving average*. By plotting this separate *MA* alongside the *MACD*, it can be used to accurately chart when momentum is shifting. A standard form of this process uses an *MA* calculated with a nine period average of the *MACD* values. When plotted together, these provide what is known as a *trigger line* or *signal line* as the points at which the two cross can be used to effectively provide transaction signals.

Example - MACD

8.5 Relative Strength Index

The *Relative Strength Index* (*RSI*) is a ratio which can be used to determine whether the market is showing signs of being *over-bought* or *over-sold*. It is a technical indicator that compares the levels of recent gains against the levels of recent losses, in order to ascertain current market conditions.

The *RSI* is calculated using the following formula:

$$RSI = 100 - 100/1 + RS*$$

*RS=Average of x days' up closes / Average of x days' down closes.

The *RSI* produces a figure relative to 100. *RSI* figures of below 30 suggest *oversold* market conditions whereas figures above 70 typically indicate *overbought* market conditions.

Trading Strategy: *RSI* can be used to determine potential reversals in price movement, as a response to either the *oversold* or *overbought* conditions occurring in the market. For example, when prices are trending downward with falling values and the *RSI* suggests a figure of below 30, this can indicate that the currency has been *oversold* and has become *undervalued*. As such, it is possible that a reversal in trend could be imminent as traders realise that prices have become relatively cheap and restart buying.

The *RSI* is also a very useful tool for confirming whether an upward or downward trend has begun to form. Where there is a possible upward trend, then the *RSI* should show a figure of above 50 in support, whereas in a possible downward trend the figure should be below 50.

Key Lesson: Large swings in the market can result in a misleading *RSI*, so it is important to be aware of this and to simultaneously use other indicators to reinforce *RSI* trade signals.

8.6 Stochastic Oscillator

The *stochastic oscillator* is another technical indicator that again provides insights into price momentum, particularly in relation to market conditions, where a currency becomes either overbought or oversold. It provides an indication, suggesting when there may be a potential reversal of price, owing to a currency becoming either under, or overvalued.

A *stochastic indicator* compares the current closing price against the price range over a given period of time. The idea behind this being that, in an upward trend, prices tend to close nearer to the highs of that session and in a downward trend prices tend to close nearer to the lows of a session.

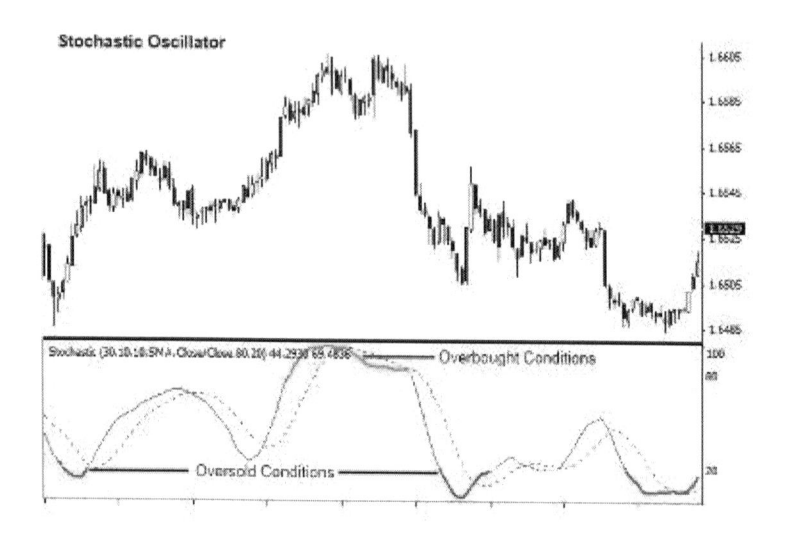

It is not essential to understand the formula for calculating the *stochastic oscillator* due to its complexity, but you should be aware that charting software will generally plot the resulting representation as two lines on a separate section under the main chart in your software. These can be used to analyse when the market is in overbought or oversold conditions, and, as such, when a reversal of trend may be expected.

Trading Strategy: When the two lines of the *stochastic oscillator* read above 80 then this is a good signal that the currency has been overbought and that a reversal to a downward trend can be expected to occur. When the two lines of the *stochastic oscillator* are below 20 on the chart then the opposite is true and it is likely that the currency has become oversold and undervalued.

8.7 Parabolic SAR Indicator

The *parabolic indicator* is a technical analysis tool that uses a method called *stop and reverse* or *SAR* as a means of determining where to place entry and exit orders.

Whilst the indicator can be complicated to calculate, it is extremely simple to understand and use. The *parabolic SAR* is often visually illustrated in charting software using dots placed above and below the charted price, which represent points of potential reversal given the current price conditions. The dots will appear either above the price in an upward trend, or below the price in a downward trend.

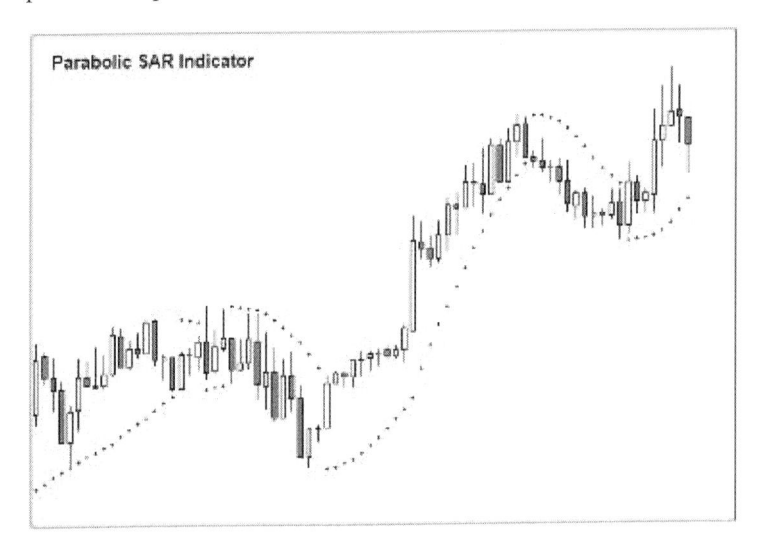

Trading Strategy: The simplicity of the *parabolic SAR* is such that, when the dots appear below the price on a chart then, they suggest a buy signal and when they are above the price line they suggest a sell signal. The positions of the dots can also be used to set trailing stop levels and to indicate when to exit a trade.

8.8 Average Direction Index

The *average direction index* (*ADX*) is another *oscillating indicator*, which is primarily used to determine the momentum present in current market conditions. Rather than trying to identify the direction of trends, the *ADX* can be used to measure the relative strength of an existing trend and whether there is the continuing momentum necessary to keep that trend going.

The *ADX* is calculated using figures from two measures of price movement, the *positive direction indicator* +*DI* that provides a measure of upward price trends and the *negative direction indicator* –*DI* that provides a measure of downward price trends.

The actual calculation of *ADX* for the purposes of this book will not be detailed. However, it is sufficient to know that the *index* itself produces a figure that will range between 1 and 100. When the *index* produces a figure of *less than 20* then it indicates that the particular trend is relatively weak, whereas when the value of the *index* is *above 40-50* then it suggests that the trend, either up or down, is relatively strong and that there is significant momentum necessary to maintain the price movement.

When the *ADX* crosses above the 40 range, but fails to remain above it for any significant period of time, then this also suggests that a trend has potentially run its course and that a reversal can be expected. When the *ADX* crosses above 20 in the index level, it often indicates that a new trend could be developing.

Key Lesson: The only problem with the *ADX* is that it does not provide an indication of whether to buy, or sell. It is, however, an extremely useful tool for determining whether a trend is strong and likely to continue, as well as, when a trend begins to subsequently weaken.

Trading Strategy: Use the *ADX* as a tool to illustrate when a particular trend is beginning to develop and when there are strengthening trends of which you are in a position to take advantage. If the *ADX* stagnates around a level of 20, then this would suggest that the price is merely ranging between confining boundaries. As the *ADX* rises above 20, then this should be taken as a signal that a new trend, either upwards, or downwards, is beginning to develop. If the *ADX* continues to push above the 40 or even 50 levels, then this can be taken as significant evidence that a trend, supported by solid momentum, is occurring. Once the *ADX* begins to range lower again, then this would be a good time to exit any trades and lock in the resulting profits.

8.9 Common Indicators – Conclusions

As we have seen *indicators* are an extremely useful set of tools that can be used to help target trade entries and exits; identify trends and price movements; and help provide reliable trading signals.

The way to use *indicators,* effectively, is to understand how the mechanisms work and what they mean in relation to the market conditions. By having an understanding of the fundamental nature of each *indicator,* then this ensures that you recognise the strengths and weaknesses of the tools and the indications they can provide.

As we have mentioned previously, successful traders will often develop trading strategies that rely upon multiple combinations of these *indicators* and use them concurrently. This, ultimately, increases the chances of the analysis providing accurate and reliable trading signals, and reduces the occasions where a profitable transaction may be missed. Multiple *indicators* should reinforce each other, strengthening trading strategy, and will especially do so when they are combined in ways that provide information on different elements of the market.

Trading Strategy: The most effective combinations should comprise *indicators* that can help identify trends mixed with those that help to determine the levels of momentum supporting that particular trend. Below are a couple of examples of how you may combine some of the more common *indicators*:

- Stochastic Indicator + Bollinger Bands
- RSI + Moving Averages

Each trader will ultimately develop their own particular combination of *indicators*. Many have searched in vain for the ultimate strategy that works every time, but the reality remains that there is no 'magic strategy' that delivers profits on each transaction. The best way to profit, from the use of *indicators,* is to learn from experience and discover how they respond to different market conditions. From this, it will then become possible to develop strategies that work for you.

Key Lesson: Charting software should be able to calculate and plot all of these *common indicators* and many others, automatically, on your behalf. It is wise to spend time learning how each *indicator* works, especially those that have not been mentioned here. They are constantly being developed, adjusted and improved. There are many resources online that can keep you updated when new indicators are published, and which will allow you to download *indicators* not included in your standard charting package.

Chapter 9: Fibonacci

Fibonacci concepts are particularly relevant to many types of technical trading, and it is important to learn and understand the importance of *Fibonacci ratios*, as they are very often applied in many trading strategies or analysis techniques. Although there are different variations of the *Fibonacci ratios* and various methods by which they can be used, there are two main methods which we will consider: *Retracement* and *extension*.

Fibonacci ratios, described simply, are sequences of numbers that tend to relate to the naturally occurring proportions between elements of the universe. Discovered by Leonardo Fibonacci, the ratios all stem from the following common number sequence: 1, 1, 2, 3, 5, 8, 13, 21, 34, 55, 89, 144...

After the first few numbers, if you were to calculate the ratios between consecutive numbers in this sequence then this would always produce a figure of 0.618. If you were to measure the ratios between alternate numbers in the sequence, then you would continually get the number 0.382. These numbers, in addition to others, are known as the *golden mean* and it is these figures which are used to derive *Fibonacci retracement* and *extension* levels throughout technical analysis of the Forex market:

Fibonacci retracement levels: 0.236, 0.382, 0.500, 0.618, 0.764
Fibonacci extension levels: 0, 0.382, 0.618, 1.000, 1.382, 1.618

Key Lesson: It is not necessary to fully understand how to calculate this sequence of numbers, merely to know that they are used regularly by traders to select and determine levels in the market, whereby it is expected that something will happen. This, in turn, means that they can be used to plan trading strategy. Charting software will calculate both *Fibonacci retracement* and *extension* numbers and apply them to your charts

Traders use the *Fibonacci retracement* figures as levels to determine areas of support and resistance. These provide information as to where to set entry and exit points and where to place stops.

Traders tend to use *Fibonacci extension* levels as a means of directing where to set profit target levels.

Because so many traders use these techniques then prices very often react in predictable ways when these levels are reached or passed.

9.1 Fibonacci Retracement

The *Fibonacci retracement* method is used to identify levels of support or resistance based upon the sequence of values mentioned earlier. It is an extremely useful tool for traders as it can identify the entry and exit positions for trades, the target prices of transactions, and where to locate stop losses.

The underlying premise of *Fibonacci retracement* is that, following a significant movement up or down in price, the new levels of support or resistance can be calculated based upon values associated with this price movement. Your trading software should have a built-in *Fibonacci retracement* tool which will plot horizontal lines on a chart to represent the levels of support or resistance calculated using the key ratios – 23.6%, 38.2%, 50%, 61.8%, and 100%.

Key Lesson: The *retracement* tool works best in a trending market. It follows that, in an upward price swing, you should **buy** at the *retracement support levels* and that in a downward trending market, you should **sell** at the *retracement resistance levels*.

9.2 Fibonacci Extension

Fibonacci extension is a tool that extends the *Fibonacci* levels beyond the standard *retracement* 100% level and calculates new potential levels of support and resistance.

Chapter 10: Trading Cycle

The fact that repeated patterns often develop, within currency price movements, is the fundamental basis of technical analysis and technical trading methods. One pattern that is very important to understand and learn is the basic *trading cycle*. By knowing how the *trading cycle* works and often develops, it becomes possible to recognise where the price movement is within the cycle. This, in turn, can guide trading strategy by providing useful signposts relating to when and where trade entry and exit points should be set. An understanding of the price cycle sequence will also help improve the use of trading tools, such as indicators and oscillators.

The basic *trading cycle* can be seen in the diagram below:

Key Lesson: In reality the *trading cycle* rarely develops in such a uniform pattern, and with such regularity, but it is important to understand the basic elements of the cycle.

The *trading cycle* also forms the basis for a number of more complex price pattern analysis theories: The *Elliot wave pattern* and *Harmonic wave patterns*.

Chapter 11: Advanced Chart Patterns

The aim of all technical analysis is the early identification of patterns that have the potential to provide an indication as to where the price of a currency may be moving in the near or longer-term future. In addition to the chart patterns that have already been seen, there are many additional analysis techniques that can be used to predict price movements over longer periods of time. These types of analysis tend to consider the patterns of *price cycles* and *wave patterns* that appear with predictable regularity within currency movements.

11.1 Elliott Wave Theory

The *Elliott wave theory* is a concept developed by Ralph Nelson Elliott in the 1920s, which, although first applied to stock market fluctuations, can be similarly applied to the technical analysis currencies.

The theory, behind the *wave pattern*, challenges the historical idea that financial markets move in chaotic patterns and replaces this with the theory that markets actually fluctuate in *repetitive patterns* or *cycles*. These tend to be directly related to the influences affecting traders, at any particular time, and to the related mass psychology of market participants. Elliott discovered that, the upward, or downward, swings in market prices tend to respond to this mass psychology producing similar *repeated patterns* over different periods of time, which he categorised as *waves*.

The *Elliott wave pattern* is an in depth analysis of these particular waves, which works using *fractals*. These are essentially mathematically elements that will infinitely repeat themselves on a constantly reducing scale, or simply, a pattern within a pattern within a pattern. By using *fractals* Elliott was able to suggest that financial markets are structured in the same way, producing repeated patterns, which, over time, become predictable.

Elliott determined an *impulsive wave*, i.e. one which moves with the predominate trend, has five main elements which should be unique and identifiable. He also suggested that, in each of these five waves, it should be further possible to identify a structure formed from the same pattern but on a smaller scale. This, in theory, should be continually repeated over smaller and smaller scales reflecting the *fractal* structure.

Price movements can be reduced into trends, corrections and sideways movement, and it is the relationship between these factors that generates the *Elliott wave pattern*. Elliott determined that, following an upward or downward trend, there is always a correction which produces some movement that is contra-trend. He named the upward/downward trend element of the pattern as *impulsive waves* and the correcting movement as *corrective waves*.

These elements form a wave pattern that Elliott named the *5-3 wave pattern*. Broken down, this means that a complete cycle of the *Elliott wave* should consist of 5 movements that follow the direction of the prevailing trend, followed by *3 corrective* movements that will move against the direction of the trend.

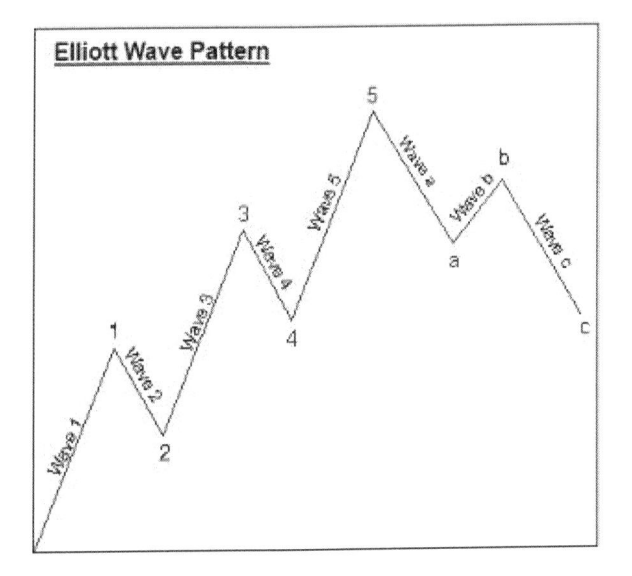

This type of *wave pattern* is more difficult to identify through technical analysis than some of the earlier patterns considered. However, it is an important pattern to be aware of. With experience, this type of pattern becomes much easier to recognise as will the trading opportunities that it can present.

Key Lesson: It is important to remember that the concept behind the *Elliott wave theory* is based on *fractals* therefore, the *5-3 pattern* can be seen repeated in ever smaller elements and can be observed over many different timeframes.

11.2 Harmonic Wave Patterns

Another useful category of advanced chart patterns are known as *harmonic wave patterns*. A number of which are discussed below:

11.3 ABCD Pattern

The *ABCD pattern* can appear in either a bullish or bearish situation, where *AB* and *CD* are known as the legs whilst the *BC* segment is known as the *correction* or *retracement*. The size of each segment is related to *Fibonacci retracement values*. From the *AB* segment, the subsequent *BC* segment should reach the 0.618 level, followed by the *CD* segment reaching the 1.272 level. As the pattern is completed then the indication is that the price is set for a reversal, thus suggesting an opportunity to either buy or sell depending on whether the pattern has been observed in a bullish or bearish trend.

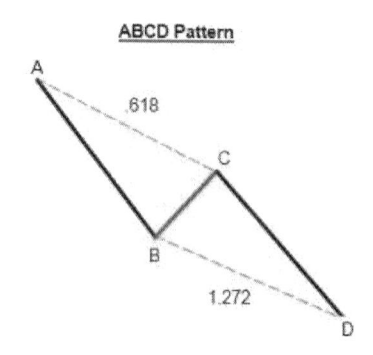

ABCD Pattern

Key Lesson: The reliability of the *ABCD* pattern increases when the distance and time intervals between *AB* and *CD* are of a similar value.

11.4 Three-Drive Pattern

The *three-drive pattern* is very similar to the *ABCD pattern*. The main difference is that this pattern is represented by three main segments called *drives* and two retracement segments. Again, the pattern relates to the key Fibonacci retracement values.

As with the *ABCD pattern* it is important to let the full *three-drive pattern* complete before taking responsive trading action.

Key Lesson: The reliability of this pattern increases when the time and distances of the retracement segments are of similar values, and when the second and third drives are of similar intervals.

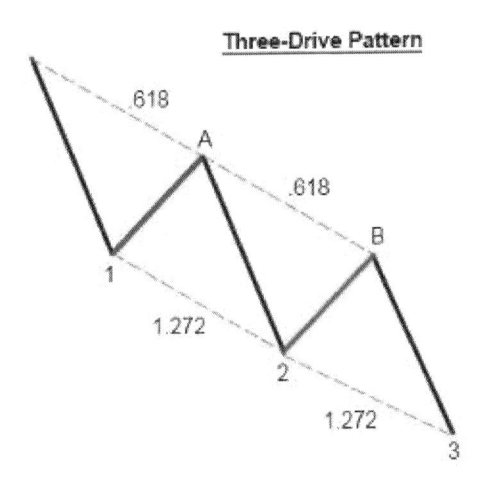

Three-Drive Pattern

11.5 Other Harmonic Patterns

There are a number of other *harmonic price patterns* that can be effectively used to predict and indicate retracements and reversals. Each has a specific pattern that develops over time, and it can be extremely useful to be aware of each. The diagrams, below, highlight some of the more common of these harmonic patterns:

Gartley Pattern

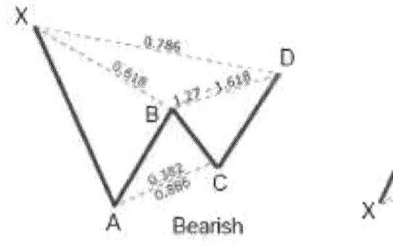

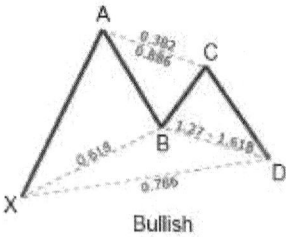

Bearish / Bullish

Bat Pattern

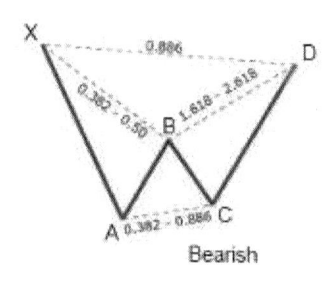

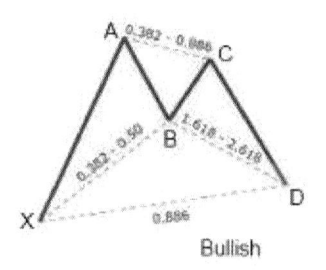

Bearish / Bullish

Butterfly Pattern

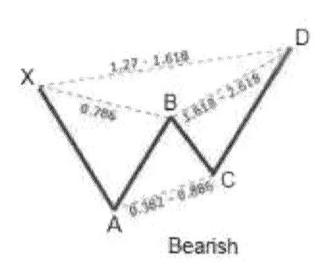

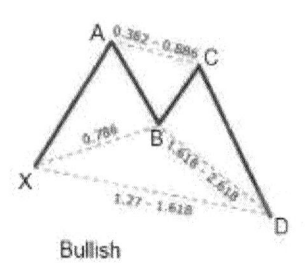

Bearish / Bullish

Key Lesson: With *harmonic wave patterns* it is important to always ensure that the full pattern completes before taking a related trading position.

Chapter 12: Timeframes

In order to successfully trade Forex, it is extremely important to understand the nature and relevance of *timeframes*. This is because the market reacts differently depending upon the period of time over which activity is occurring. All charting software allows you to monitor and display different *timeframes*: 1 min, 5 min, 10 min, 1 hour, 4 hours, 1 day, etc. Traders will use different *timeframes* to look for 'opportunity' in the market.

Deciding which *timeframe* to use is very much dependent upon individual preference and it will generally reflect conditions such as personality, trading goals, and personal strategy. Long-term investors may often be satisfied to only consider daily, or longer period price charts, whereas day traders will need to use multiple *timeframes* in order to maximise the possible trading opportunities.

Choosing the *timeframes* you wish to use as a basis for your trading strategy will depend upon your individual requirements, but there are some general guidelines relating to how the various *timeframes* perform, that should be considered.

Shorter timeframes like the 'one' or 'five' minute charting periods' are extremely frenetic in nature. Movement happens very quickly with prices fluctuating rapidly, sometimes with no discernable trend. As a trader you must be constantly alert as to when to move in and out of individual trades. The volatile nature of shorter time periods can be extremely stressful to understand and interpret, and, as such, are often more suited to seasoned traders.

A *medium-term timeframe* such as the one-hour chart period provides a less stressful environment, as movement is often less rapid but still provides sufficient opportunities for regular trading activity. The additional length of the session means that, as a beginner, you have more time to interpret and analyse the data and then to make subsequent trading decisions.

Key Lesson: The only way to truly become comfortable with *timeframes* is to practise using a combination of them and to then decide which can work best for you.

One point to consider is that shorter *timeframe* trading often requires less capital and can allow you to take greater advantage of leverage, it also often allows you to utilise tighter stop losses. Trading over longer *timeframes* will often require greater available capital to cover potential swings in the market.

12.1 Multiple Timeframes

Using only one *timeframe* can result in misleading analysis. For example, a trader using a 5 minute chart for a particular currency pair may decide that their analysis suggests evidence of a rising market. However, another trader looking at the same currency pair using a one hour *timeframe* may see that the market is actually in an overall downward trend. This is why it is important to employ the concept of *multiple timeframes*.

By using more than one *timeframe*, it becomes possible to gain a greater understanding of what is happening across the whole of the market. In practice, this often means selecting a *primary timeframe* which will act as the foundation for your trading strategy. For example, should you decide to use a 10 minute chart as a *primary timeframe*, you would use this as the basis for plotting all your relevant technical analyses and indicators to identify trends and trading opportunities. You would then support this *primary timeframe* with additional *supporting timeframes*. These should consist of one *shorter timeframe* - 1 minute chart, and two *longer timeframes* - 1 hour and 4 hour charts. Most charting software will allow you to display multiple charts, side by side, on screen, which makes comparison relatively easy. Analysis of the *supporting timeframes* should help to determine whether there is corroborating evidence that reinforces any conclusions you have made relating to the activity present in the *primary timeframe*. This should improve your understanding of how the market is behaving in its entirety, and aid the accuracy of decisions.

Chapter 13: Trading Strategy

13.1 Breakouts

As well as looking for trends in the market, one of the elements that a trader should constantly be looking for is the *breakout*. *Breakouts* occur when the price passes through a level of support or resistance and continues to move in that particular direction. This type of activity can be produced as a result of many different events and will present as either a continuation of a preceding trend, or as the start of a new trend. When true *breakouts* develop, there is often a rush of trading activity as traders seek to capitalise on the movement, and this, in itself, often pushes the price further in the new direction.

In a period of consolidation they occur as a *continuance breakout* forming in the direction of the preceding trend. Prices can also *breakout* at the beginning of a new trend, if there is a reversal. Alternatively, when prices are ranging between two bounding support or resistance levels then *breakouts* can occur in, either the upward or downward directions.

In order to effectively trade a *breakout*, it is first necessary to determine whether there is an actual *breakout* occurring, or whether there are conditions causing misleading price movements that could be misinterpreted as a *breakout*. Using multiple combinations of charting techniques, technical analysis, and, fundamental analysis, will help to identify reliable *breakout signals*.

Key Lesson: *Breakouts* are more likely to occur during periods of high volume, when there are greater numbers of participants in the market. Higher volume levels will mean that, when a *breakout* begins, there is substantial supporting activity which helps sustain the *breakout* and perpetuates price movement.

As there is no comprehensive measure of volume available in the Forex market, it can make the process of spotting high volume periods difficult. *Volatility* is therefore the key to identifying when there is an increase in market participants and, as such, when there is the potential support for a particular *breakout*. If there is a large price movement in a relatively short period of time, then price volatility can be said to be high, conversely, where there are small price movements over short time periods, then this can be classed as a period with relatively low volatility.

Trading Strategy: Many traders will get sucked into a *breakout* as it is happening, and try and follow the rapid/volatile movement. The problem with this type of trading is that, by the very nature of the high volatility, it can mean that any profits can be rapidly reduced if prices move against your position. Therefore, a much more effective way to profit from *breakouts*, is to look for currency pairs where there is initially relatively little volatility. By doing so, you give yourself sufficient time to analyse the market conditions and the technical nature of the price movements, and as a result put in place trades that will allow you to benefit when a *breakout* does occur. This means that you have a better opportunity of benefiting from being in at the start of the *breakout* and you may dictate the terms of your trade, rather than trying to chase a *breakout* that is already well underway.

13.2 Measuring Volatility

A number of techniques can be used to measure the *volatility* in prices. Essentially, any technical measure employed should be used to try to determine the level of price movement taking place within a given time period. Of the technical analysis methods we have considered previously, both the *bollinger bands* and the *moving average* indicators are suited to providing a measure of *volatility*.

In the case of *bollinger bands*, the bands will tighten closer to the central moving average when there is *low price volatility*, whereas the bands will broaden away from the central moving average when there is *high price volatility*.

Moving averages can also provide a good indication of *volatility* as they indicate the average price over a given period of time.

13.3 Confirming a Breakout

As mentioned previously, *breakout signals* don't always lead to a true *breakout* event developing. Over time, if you traded all these false signals then this would likely result in significant losses. However, there are ways to help improve the chances of spotting and confirming true *breakouts*. It is possible to use some of the methods described earlier to determine when a breakout is more likely. They can also indicate the degree of momentum in the market at any particular time, which provides a good measure of where the price may be ultimately heading.

The *moving average convergence and divergence indicator* (*MACD*) is a very good measure of price and market momentum. When the *MACD* histogram is relatively small, it suggests low levels of momentum, whereas when the *MACD* histogram is larger, it suggests greater levels of momentum. The way this works in relation to trends, is that when a trend is occurring and the *MACD* is high then this tends to indicate high levels of momentum and strong support for that trend. However, when the *MACD* indicator registers low momentum in a trending scenario, then this often indicates that support for that trend is subsiding.

The *relative strength indicator* (*RSI*) is another good measure of divergence, providing useful information as to when the market is showing signs of either being in *over-bought* or *over-sold* conditions. In both these situations, when they happen, it is often a good signal that there may be an imminent change in forthcoming trend patterns.

13.4 Trading the Opposite Break

Due to the nature of the Forex market, many potential breakouts fail to become true breakouts, instead, prices swing in the opposite direction to that which was expected. Many traders refer to these situations as a *fake out* and the opposite price movement that results as *fadeout*.

The reason for these *fake outs* often comes from the inherent differences between the trading activities of *institutional traders* (market makers) and *retail traders* (market participants). At this stage, it is not necessary to know all of the intricacies that lead to these *fadeouts* as, over time and with experience, you will learn to identify when they are occurring and why.

It is prudent though to remember that they do happen, and that often they will occur within ranging markets at times when chart patterns have suggested a change in trend. This is because institutional investors are well aware that many of the chart patterns we have described are readily known and used amongst retail traders. This means that there is a degree of predictability in terms of what may happen, at any given time, in the marketplace. This predictability can be used by market makers to push prices in the opposite direction to that which the majority of retail participants may be expecting, resulting in a significant windfall for them.

It is essential for a novice trader to be aware of *fake outs* and to always understand that the market can react in a different manner to that which is expected. Ultimately, this knowledge helps to improve trading strategy as it means a trader must ensure that they use multiple buy signals and price indicators before making trades, and understand the necessary use of stop losses and trailing stops, in order to lock in profits and prevent damage from any swings in price.

13.5 Divergence Trading

One of the problems for any trader of Forex is deciding when to enter the market and when to exit the market. Knowing when a price is likely to reverse, and getting out of a trade prior to that point, is vital to lock-in profits. *Divergence trading* is one of the methods that can be used to help improve the planning and execution of trades in order to increase overall gains.

Divergence trading involves the comparison of actual price movement in relation to an indicator. Indicators can provide three different types of trading signal: *Crossing over a major signal line*; *Crossing over a centre line*; and *Indicator divergence*.

Indicator divergence occurs when the actual price movement and an indicator are travelling in opposite directions. *Positive divergence* refers to situations when the price is in a downward trend and the indicator (*MACD, RSI, and Stochastic Oscillator*) is moving in the opposite upward direction. N*egative divergence* describes when the price is an upward trend whilst the indicator is moving downwards.

Key Lesson: *Divergence* is a useful early signal of possible price reversal, and, as such, when used properly can work well as a reliable *leading indicator*.

Divergence often happens over longer periods of time, so it is useful to employ trend lines, and support/resistance levels as a means of analysing the market over the short-term, which should provide additional evidence for a reversal occurring.

The philosophy behind *divergence trading* is that, consistently, price and momentum tend to work together e.g. higher prices are often supported by higher levels of momentum, and conversely lower prices are often supported by lower momentum levels. When there is a divergence of these two elements in opposing directions then this signifies that the price movement is losing momentum and that there must be a correction coming at some point in the near future, most probably resulting in a reversal.

Trading Strategy: By knowing how price and indicators interact, *divergence* provides vital signals that suggest when a trend may be beginning to weaken. *Divergence* can be used as a reliable leading indicator, providing trade signals, which take advantage of changes in market momentum or price direction.

There are two types of *divergence*: *Regular divergence* and *Hidden divergence*.

Regular divergence is best used as an indicator signalling the end of an existing trend or that a reversal should be expected. In practice, it means that even where the price is continuing to head upwards or downwards on trend, the evidence of *divergence* is highlighting that momentum is beginning to slow and that the support for the increasing or decreasing value is starting to reduce. Where the price is high, but the indicator/oscillator moves lower, then this is known as *regular bearish divergence*, and often indicates the top of a price run. Conversely, when the price is continuing to move lower, but momentum begins to swing higher, this is known as *regular bullish divergence*, and often corresponds with prices reaching the bottom of a trend.

Hidden divergence occurs actually within a trend and can be used as a signal to suggest that the trend will continue. *Hidden **bullish** divergence* can be seen when the actual price is registering progressively higher lows, but the oscillator is, conflictingly, showing lower lows. When this particular combination is found in an upward trend, then it suggests *hidden divergence* and suggests evidence of continued support for that trend.

*Hidden **bearish** divergence* will be seen in a downward trend and occurs when the price makes progressively lower highs whilst the indicator/oscillator is showing higher highs. This can be taken to mean a continuation of the prevailing trend.

13.5.1 Divergence - Conclusion

Evidence of *divergences* should not be used solely as a means of determining when and where to enter transactions. They instead should primarily be employed as a supporting factor among other technical analysis tools. By building an understanding of *divergences* into your analysis process, it will help to spot profitable occasions and to generate a clearer picture of market conditions and activity.

Key Lesson: As with any form of trading that relies upon technical analysis, if, at any point, you are unsure as how the price activity may be developing, then it is sensible to wait and see how things progress, even if, at times, this means missing out on opportunities that would have resulted in profits.

13.6 Scalping

Scalping is a technique often employed by traders of stock market securities whereby they attempt to make a relatively small profit from hundreds of trades made in the course of a day. By *scalping* a trader hopes to exploit the differences between the bid/ask prices or profit from very small negative or positive movements in price.

Chapter 14: The Carry Trade

The *carry trade* is a particular trading strategy that can allow you to profit by simply holding a currency for a period of time, even when there is no significant movement in the actual price of that currency.

Basically, the *carry trade* exploits differences in interest rates of one currency over another, in order to profit from the differential. To achieve this in practice, the *carry trade* relies upon the borrowing or selling of one currency with a low interest rate, then using this to purchase a currency that is yielding a higher interest rate. Whilst you are paying the lower interest rate on the currency you have borrowed, you collect the higher interest rate on the currency you have purchased. The difference between the two signifies a profit even when the price positions have remained flat.

A simple example of this would be: Consider if you were able to go to a bank and secure a loan for $10,000 at a rate of 2% and you then took this money and were able to put it in a savings account that paid 6%. You are essentially receiving a profit of 4% on the trade. However, in reality, banks make this extremely difficult to do as they nearly always keep lending rates above those of the savings rate. The *carry trade*, therefore, is a very useful method of producing profits for financial traders and through Forex it can be a particularly profitable trading technique.

14.1 Forex Carry Trade

In the Forex market a number of factors make the *carry trade* a very useful instrument for traders. When you buy a currency pair e.g. GBP/USD then you are actually buying the British Pound and selling the US dollar, at the same time you pay interest on the currency that you buy and receive interest on the currency that you sell. The unique nature of the Forex spot market means that interest payments are paid every day, based upon the position held for that day. Brokers will close and reopen your position every night and, subsequently, credit or debit interest, based upon the difference between the currency pair that you hold.

Key Lesson: The influence of leverage means that interest rates can be rapidly multiplied over time.

Trading Strategy: The following example illustrates how the *carry trade* can practically be applied to Forex spot markets, and the resulting outcomes. It also accounts for the influence of leverage and how this can begin to significantly increase potential gains.

If you had $10,000 in your account and decided to place $1,000 of that on a margin, at a leverage of 100:1 you could potentially control $100,000 of currency. A broker requiring only 1% margin will hold this $1,000 as collateral on the trade. You now decide to invoke a *carry trade*. You identify a currency pair (e.g. GBP/USD) that has an interest rate differential of 4%; you take a position and decide to maintain the trade for a period of one year. Over the course of the year, even if there is very little movement in price between the two currencies, then the trade would result in a return on your investment of 4%, providing you with a profit of $4,000. When this return is considered in relation to your initial account fund of $10,000 then you have received the equivalent of a 40% return on your investment. Even if the currency price drops over the period, you can set stops, in order to minimise any potential losses. If the currency pair rises over the period then you also collect the capital growth in addition to the interest payments.

To summarise, the potential outcomes of the *carry trade* in these circumstances, the following may occur:

Outcome 1 - The price of the currency pair loses value – if the level of this loss reaches the price set-aside by the margin, then the position would be closed. By setting stop losses, then capital losses can be reduced.

Outcome 2 - The price of the currency pair remains the same. In this case, then there is little or no capital growth or loss, but interest is still paid. On the previous example, this would represent a return of 40% on the initial investment of $10,000 or $4,000.

Outcome 3 - The price of the currency pair rises – if the value of the pair rises during the period of the investment, then not only is interest paid over the lifetime of the trade, but you will also receive capital growth relative to the price increase.

Key Lesson: You should also be aware that the *carry trade* can equally operate in the opposite direction. Therefore, in the earlier example, if you had sold the British pound rather than buying, and bought the US dollar as opposed to selling, the result after the year would not have been a profitable *carry trade* yielding 4% but instead, would have resulted in a *negative carry*, meaning a loss of 4%. It is therefore very important to continually monitor fluctuations in interest rates applicable to any currency you hold, as this will ensure that you continue to receive revenue as opposed to paying to hold a position.

14.2 Setting up the Carry Trade

The first thing to do when setting up a *carry trade* is to obtain the interest rates for all relevant currencies. There are many resources available, particularly online that can provide accurate and up to date information for interest rate levels. Once you have found a pair that will yield a significant differential between the two rates, then this can provide the basis for the trade.

It is prudent to apply all the skills of technical analysis in order to establish whether the currency pair identified is in an upward trend. This will help ensure that the market will be moving in a profitable direction during the course of your trade. These skills can equally be used to identify when to execute the trade and where to set any stop losses.

Finally, it is necessary to manage the *risk* associated with the trade by limiting the percentage of your capital employed to no more than a 10% margin. As the trade will be active over the course of a year, then this level should provide a suitably sufficient risk-to-reward ratio.

Monitor the trade and interest rates closely over the course of the year to try and ensure that you are prepared to take action should it be required.

Key Lesson: The *carry trade* works best when there is a good long-term economic outlook related to the currency that is paying the interest. This is necessary because, when there is strong economic activity central banks will often raise interest rates in order to curb buying inflation. For you as an investor in that currency, this means a higher return. By contrast, when there is less economic confidence for the outlook of a currency, then investors are more likely to place their money in safer places that pay lower interest rates, but which are considered more reliable currencies. As such, this can result in less market activity associated with the riskier currency, causing the underlying price to fall. Therefore, always be aware of the economic conditions affecting your trades and be ready to act accordingly.

Chapter 15: Ready to Trade

15.1 The Forex Trading Community

In the past, the market information available to individual retail traders was limited, however, with the advent of modern media and the internet, retail Forex traders now have a wealth of information available that previously would only be known to large institutional investors.

Making good use of this available information should dramatically increase your chances of success. There are online communities, websites, blogs, etc all devoted to providing regular detailed information. These sources are extremely useful for providing new strategy ideas, highlighting trading opportunities, and generally providing a huge resource of support to help with day-to day trading.

15.2 Trading and Charting Software

Most brokers, especially those with an online presence, will provide clients with access to trading and charting software designed to facilitate the trading process. Some brokers use their own trading platforms, whilst others will provide access to generic software applications. All should include the key components that have been mentioned in this book. Additional features will become more and more relevant as you increase your trading knowledge.

You should learn how to use the *trading platform* well before making actual trades. Many brokers will provide a demonstration version of their software and it is wise to use this to develop a comprehensive understanding of how the application works and discover all the relevant features. You will be able to place and execute trading transactions in a similar manner to the real trading platform, but with the demonstration version you are provided with a helpful, risk-free, environment to practise all the skills you have acquired. A demonstration account can equally be used once you begin trading as a tool for testing trading strategy without risking personal capital.

All trading platforms should include charting features, and it is important to understand how to manipulate the software in order to display the charts you require, with the information you need. You should also learn how to apply technical analysis tools, such as trend lines, indicators, oscillators, etc, and have the software present the information on your charts.

15.3 Types of Trader

There are many different categories into which Forex traders can fall, and these tend to be determined by the individual strategies used by different traders. It may be that you decide to try a number of different techniques within your overall strategy, so it is important to know the types of trading available to you.

Scalp trader

Scalp trading is an extremely short-term strategy, which requires making lots of trades over short periods of time (minutes rather than hours). The idea is to *scalp* a relatively small profit off the many trades made during the course of the day.

It is an extremely frenetic method of trading and requires individuals who can devote all day to watching charts and rapidly placing orders based around short-term trends, highlighted by technical analysis techniques.

Day trader

A day trader tends to be an individual using short-term trading strategy, which often consists of making only one or two trades during the course of a day. It will require analysing the market in the morning and deciding upon a position to take for the day, then continuing to monitor the trades, before closing the positions as the day ends.

Day traders tend to rarely hold positions open overnight. The day will finish with the knowledge that either a profit or loss has been achieved.

Swing Trader

Swing trading is a medium-term trading strategy, where positions will be held for two to three days in order to take advantage of more defined trends. This type of trading strategy is well suited to traders who are unable to monitor markets during the day, but are able to analyse and plan trades in the evening and then place orders that will last over the medium-term. This means it is a strategy well suited to people trading part-time or casually.

Key Lesson: With *swing trading* chances are that the market will move against you, at some point, whilst the position is held. It is therefore important to set stop losses with large margins – in order to prevent trades from closing prematurely.

This type of trading also requires strong nerves, in order to accept the fluctuations that will occur during the lifetime of each trade.

Position Trader

Position trading is a longer-term strategy that will see trades held for weeks or months. It is a type of trading that demands patience and strong nerves, as it is likely that there will be significant swings in both directions during the course of the trade.

Key Lesson: Position trading requires good knowledge and understanding of the *fundamentals* in order to predict where a currency is likely to be heading over the longer term.

15.4 Developing a Trading Plan

Once you have decided the type and style of trading that suits your particular requirements, it is necessary to develop a trading strategy that works for you. The starting point for this should be the development of a *trading plan*.

This should be the blueprint by which you manage the way you trade, the tools you use, and the analysis employed. Essentially, it should bring together everything learnt prior to trading in order to provide a comprehensive plan of how you intend to trade. The *trading plan* should comprise a series of instructions and guidelines which will help negotiate the ups and downs of trading.

Key Lesson: When trading it can be very difficult to remove emotion from the decision making process, and the stress or excitement of making or losing money will only add to this problem. A *trading plan* will help you to make decisions based upon your own predetermined processes, thus reducing the chance of making emotional mistakes.

The *plan* should not be a singular strategy, instead, it should include multiple strategies designed to take advantage of different opportunities and different market conditions. It should also contain research, analysis techniques, and most importantly the processes that need to be undertaken every time you trade.

To achieve an effective *trading plan*, you should develop a step-by-step set of processes or guidelines that you will follow before, during and after each placement of an order.

Elements that should be incorporated into the *trading plan* include:

- **Define** your trading profile

- **Determine** how you want to trade and the goals you hope to achieve

- Set **profit targets**

- **Decide** how often and when you will trade

- Decide upon a **risk profile** that suits your requirements

- Determine the steps necessary in each trade to **minimise risk**

- Put in place methods to **record** progress, as this will help determine whether goals can be achieved

-Determine your **capital risks**, i.e. how much money do you have available to trade with, and can afford to lose?

-Decide on the **timeframes** you intend to use and how trading these will fit into your lifestyle

Key Lesson: There are a number of essential elements that all trading plans should incorporate, these include: Managing personal expectations; developing a personal trading profile; risk management; setting trading rules; deciding upon a trading routine; and planning trading strategies/systems/setups.

15.5 Trading Routine

A critical part of the trading plan is developing a *trading routine*. Over time it is likely that this will become second nature to you, but it is important, initially, to plan the steps that you intend to take before trading each day. There are certain pieces of information that should be monitored every day that will influence your trading decisions. These include:

-Review open positions, and make any necessary adjustments

-Check the daily news and note any diary events that may influence your trades

-Review the trades from the previous day, and evaluate profits/losses

-Note any new setup ideas

-Identify any news or events that could cause significant market activity

-Review market sentiment

-Prepare setups and strategy for the day ahead

Key Lesson: *Trading routine* will be different for everyone and should be developed to suit individual needs and requirements. The main consideration should be that it sufficiently prepares you for the trading of the day ahead.

15.6 Trading Tools

A vital requirement of any trading plan is deciding upon the tools that will be used to analyse and execute trades. This means choosing the trading setups and strategy that are best suited to particular conditions, and deciding upon the correct analysis techniques to use in order to appropriately diagnose how and when trading should be undertaken.

15.7 Trading Discipline

The truth is that many of the setups that are available commercially as well as those that are developed individually do provide significant opportunities for success, and if used properly can allow a trader to make profitable gains. The most important thing to remember, however, when using any predetermined system of trading, is that it is critical to maintain *trading discipline*. This simply means decide on a plan and stick to it!

Key Lesson: There will be many occasions where it will be tempting to dynamically alter a setup as a situation develops. Whilst at times this can prove to be successful, or be necessary in order to deal with the unexpected, by continually changing elements of a trading setup, you considerably increase the risk of failure, over the long term.

15.8 Trading Diary

Another good idea for any trader is to develop your own individual trading diary. This will act as a road map, which you can use to plan and develop trading strategies based around events that are likely to happen in the future.

A good trading diary will take into account different trading timeframes, breaking down events into those that are expected to occur that day, over the course of the week, or over the longer-term.

There are many good online resources that provide trading diaries, but it is best if you are able to integrate the news and events listed in these, into your own diary. This will then become an essential day-to-day tool that will make sure that you aware of news and events as they are due to happen, allowing you to plan accordingly.

Key Lesson: Maintaining a good up to date *trading diary* will help ensure that you can effectively plan how, and when, to trade during the course of the day, week, or month.

The type of information to record should include:

- Potential trading opportunities

- Trigger points

- Target values

- Position sizes

- Your trade management rules

It is often difficult to continue to maintain a *trading diary*, particularly when trading frequently, but, where possible if you can stick with it, it will prove to be an extremely useful source of information and help manage trading activity.

15.9 Trading Journal

A *trading journal* should provide a record of all your trading activity. Ideally, it should be designed in such a way that not only does it provide a historically documentation of all trades and the relevant outcomes of those trades, but it should also provide the basis for building new trading strategy and improving investment setup.

Essentially, this process should make it possible to learn from both successes, and failures, in order to help advance trading outcomes. Record when trades go wrong as this will help identify where you think problems may have occurred and how these can be minimised going forward.

The information stored in a *trading journal* will be different from person to person, but there are some essential pieces of information that should always be recorded, which include: Ideas and news that provide trading ideas; market movements and potential movements; market observations; observed influential factors-and the responses to them; entry and exit triggers; order sizes; trade management rules; and, trade evaluations.

Maintaining a *trading journal* overtime will produce a great source of information that will help influence the development of future strategy, define trade management rules, and should help to shape your trading plans.

Chapter 16: Trading Systems

All trading systems work in a similar manner, they should be designed to look for and **identify a developing trend**, then apply systematic procedures to **analyse data** in a way that either proves or disproves the original findings. Each system should then **identify suitable order entry triggers**, and **propose possible profit targets**. A system should also **apply trade management techniques** to help **set stop losses, exit triggers**, and continually analyse the trade as it develops dynamically.

There are many trading strategies available and it is easy to find descriptions of these either online or from conventional resources. The best process for developing strategies and trading setups is to take these ideas and then build upon them as you develop greater levels of experience. By testing individual setup ideas in charting software and demonstration accounts it is possible to determine those that fit well with your particular style of trading and to perfect how the setup works in real conditions.

Trading Strategy: It is equally possible to develop your own individual and unique strategies, by following a few simple steps:

1. **Timeframe**. It is important to first decide the timeframe for which you will hold the trade. This will be dependent upon individual trading styles, and investment expectations. Knowing this will allow you to set charting software to display the relevant timeframe, in order to monitor the trade.

During the course of any trade it will be necessary to also monitor other timeframes, as these will help illustrate what is happening in the wider market.

2. Find indicators that help **identify a new trend**. As we have seen in the technical analysis section of this book, there are many techniques and tools which can be employed to help identify and highlight when a new trend is developing. An example of this would be the use of moving averages. Most traders will utilise a long and a

short moving average, and then use the points at which these intersect as a means of determining when new trends are beginning to form. (See moving averages and moving average crossovers).

3: Use indicators to help **confirm the trend**. Once one set of indicators has identified a possible new trend then it is necessary to try and confirm the validity of that trend, using additional indicators and analysis techniques. Examples of indicators that could be used for trend confirmation include: RSI, MACD, and Stochastic indicators.

4: **Manage the risk**. Having identified a trading opportunity, the next step is determining the trade order that should be placed and manage the risk associated with that order. This means deciding on how much account capital should be used e.g. 1%, 2%, etc and calculating the possible risk/reward ratios.

5: **Calculate/Identify entry and exit points** (triggers). As we have seen in earlier sections, one of the critical elements of Forex trading, that ultimately comes with experience, is deciding when and where to enter and exit trades. It is important to ensure that you don't enter a trade too early in the lifetime of a new trend, as it may prove to be a false trend, equally it is not good to leave it too late, by which time the chances of profiting have been reduced.

In terms of getting the entry correct, this will really depend upon personal choice and experience. Gradually it will become easier to spot the right entry points. In terms of exiting a trade there are the options of setting a trailing stop or stop loss, which will close out the trade for you, automatically, once the predetermined levels are reached. Alternatively, you may set specific profit targets, possibly based on previous movement, which will again act as exit triggers as the price reaches those levels.

A very popular method of calculating exit triggers is to use support and resistance levels as buy or sell markers.

6: **Record the system and follow it**. One mistake that many novice traders make is failing to follow their trading system, once they get involved in the trade. This is extremely easy to do, as emotions begin to overrule good judgement, but it can also be a very costly error to make. By sticking to the system, you know what you intend to do, and should do, at each step of the trade cycle. Over time this should help ensure trades are more successful.

16.1 Risk Management

It is vital to view trading as an investment process, and not consider it as gambling. *Risk management* is the process by which financial management techniques are used to ensure that trades are made with considered methodology and that steps are put in place to reduce the chances of losing money, thus ensuring that the risk to financial capital is minimised.

The first rule of *risk management* is that you should never trade with more money than you can afford to lose. Most Forex day traders will start with an account of no less than $10,000 that they can afford to lose should the worst case occur. Whilst day trading is often seen as a great way to make additional money in hard times, many people have placed themselves in greater financial difficulty by trading with money that they really cannot afford to risk. The main problem is that if you are heavily invested in trades with money that is essential for your day-to-day living then it becomes virtually impossible to detach yourself emotionally from the investment process. This reduces trading discipline and can ultimately lead to bad investment decisions.

The next essential step of *risk management* is education. The better prepared you can be before making any trades backed by actually capital resources, the higher the chances of succeeding going forward. Reading resources, such as this, and other titles will help provide a comprehensive background to the Forex market and highlight the idiosyncrasies that will be encountered in daily trading. Having a good working knowledge of how the market operates, and the specific terminology used amongst market participants should help prevent mistakes or misinterpretations. It is also advisable to extensively use demonstration accounts and demonstration software in order to develop, understand and perfect strategies and setups prior to risking capital. There is a wealth of online and offline information sources that can help assist in learning Forex methodology.

There are also many opportunities available to gain access to mentors or tuition that promise to offer help to fast-track the Forex learning process. Many of these can be extremely beneficial as they provide the opportunity to learn directly from people with genuine Forex trading experience. These resources are likely to be fairly costly, so it is important to consider the benefits that they can provide against the capital outlay required.

16.2 Capital Management

Even when the skills and preparation are in place to begin trading, *risk management* should be an everyday consideration that is actively built into your overall trading plan.

If a trading strategy provided, on average, an 80% rate of return, it is still necessary to consider when and how those returns could occur. If an 80% return rate translates into 80 successful trades out of 100, then this also means 20 trades out of 100 have the potential to lose money. The problem is that it is impossible to predict where and when these 20 losing trades may occur. They could potentially happen consecutively, and, if this was the case, then without *capital management* procedures a losing streak like this could rapidly wipe-out the reserves in a trading account.

Key Lesson: Professional traders will put in place procedures to help minimise the risk on every trade and ensure that only a small proportion of overall capital is invested in any one position.

The following table shows the differential rates at which capital can be reduced during a losing period, depending upon the proportion of capital risked on each trade.

Trade	Capital	2% risk	Trade	Capital	10% risk
1	20,000	400	1	20,000	2,000
2	19,600	392	2	18,000	1,800
3	19,208	384	3	16,200	1,620
4	18,824	376	4	14,580	1,458
5	18,447	369	5	13,122	1,312
6	18,078	362	6	11,810	1,181
7	17,717	354	7	10,629	1,063
8	17,363	347	8	9,566	957
9	17,015	340	9	8,609	861
10	16,675	333	10	7,748	775

This shows that with just ten consecutive loss making trades the difference in overall capital reduction could be from 20,000 to 16,675 when placing trades that represent 2% of overall account capital, and from 20,000 to just 7,748 of capital left when placing trades that represent 10% of capital. That would be a loss of 3,325 in the 2% example compared with a much more substantial loss of 12,252 in the 10% example.

It is, therefore, vital to decide and plan what proportion of capital you are willing to commit to individual trades, in order to ensure that the long-term overall risks remain acceptable.

Key Lesson: It is best to only risk a small percentage of overall capital per trade, as over time this technique will ultimately ensure your account remains protected during loss making periods.

16.3 Trading Setups

All the tools, processes and concepts mentioned previously will all benefit developing how and when you will trade. We will now briefly consider two elements which are vital for everyday trading and which, used properly, will help improve the chances of success.

16.4 Stop Losses

We have suggested how *stop loss* orders should be used in relation to many of the analysis and trading techniques introduced in this book. The stop loss is an extremely important tool for any Forex trader, as they help to plan trades and execute sell or buy orders, and can be used to automate the trading process when you are unavailable.

Your use of stop losses should reflect market conditions and your particular trading strategy. They should be used in every trade you conduct. It is important to consider a number of factors when placing stop losses:

1. A *stop loss* should not be placed too tightly above or below your entry point. This is because markets will always fluctuate up and down to a certain extent, even in a clearly trending market. If the *stop loss* is set to tightly to the price then these fluctuations could easily cause the trade to close prematurely.

2. Equally, *stop losses* should not be set too far from the entry points. Getting the right balance of where to set *stop losses* will improve with experience.

3. *Stop losses* should not be placed exactly on levels of support or resistance. Instead these levels should be used as markers whereby *stop losses* can be set just above or just below these positions. As prices will tend to migrate towards support and resistance levels, this will prevent any trades closing early due to fluctuations in price.

16.5 Calculating Position Sizes

Deciding how much currency you wish to buy in any given trade is an important element of every trade. Calculating a position size will help you keep within the constraints of your own risk profile. A simple example of calculating position size can be seen below:

This example considers how to calculate a position size, where your account denomination is the same as the quote currency of the pair you wish to purchase.

You have $5,000 in a trading account and wish to use a trading system that trades EUR/USD risking about 200 pips per trade. You do not want to risk more than 1% of your account per trade.

Using the account balance and the percentage amount you want to risk, it is possible to calculate the dollar amount risked.

Firstly,

$5,000 x 1% (or 0.01) = $50

Next, divide the amount risked by the stop to find the value per pip.

($50)/ (200 pips) = $0.25/pip

Finally, multiply the value per pip by a known unit-pip value of EUR/USD. In this case, with 10,000 units (or one mini lot), each pip of movement is worth $1.

$0.25 per pip x ((10k units of EUR/USD)/ (USD 1 per pip)) = 2,500 units of EUR/USD

Therefore, you should place an order for 2,500 units of EUR/USD or less to stay within the 1% risk level.

When your account is held in the denomination of the base currency, simply convert the amount to be risked into the quote currency using the current exchange rate, before continuing with the rest of the calculation.

Getting the position size of orders correct will become easy over time, and there are many online calculators that will perform the calculations for you. Often trading software will include these tools.

Chapter 17: Some Final Thoughts

The aim of this book, throughout, has been to provide an introduction to the Foreign Exchange Markets and to provide you with the necessary tools to begin trading. One important lesson to learn is that unfortunately there is no 'perfect setup' or 'magic strategy' that will work every time. Whilst many books and websites will try and say different, suggesting that their setup is the path to 'guaranteed profits', the truth remains that there are no guarantees when it comes to trading. The markets are not simply movements of numbers, but are the dynamic expressions of human nature and of the market participants. This coupled with the difficulties of trying to predict the future makes it impossible to reduce the risks to a single calculable equation, whereby the results are consistently accurate.

Key Lesson: On occasions you will find yourself on the wrong side of the market and making incorrect decisions. This is not always a bad thing. As with everything, it is possible to learn from mistakes and to use them to help improve the chances that future decisions will be more successful.

This book is by no means an exhaustive description of the Forex markets or Forex trading. Instead the aim has been to provide you with the information necessary to understand how the markets work and to outline some of the tools and techniques that can be utilised in order to begin planning and actually making trades. Ultimately the process of trading should be a continual learning curve, with each successful and unsuccessful trade providing new insights and new ideas as to how to profit.

Printed in Great Britain
by Amazon.co.uk, Ltd.,
Marston Gate.